Donald MacDonald

South Sea Languages

A series of studies on the languages of the New Hebrides and other South Sea Islands

Donald MacDonald

South Sea Languages
A series of studies on the languages of the New Hebrides and other South Sea Islands

ISBN/EAN: 9783743408043

Manufactured in Europe, USA, Canada, Australia, Japa

Cover: Foto ©Andreas Hilbeck / pixelio.de

Manufactured and distributed by brebook publishing software (www.brebook.com)

Donald MacDonald

South Sea Languages

NEW HEBRIDES LINGUISTICS.

INTRODUCTORY.

THREE

New Hebrides Languages

(EFATESE, EROMANGAN, SANTO.)

By the REV. D^{on} MACDONALD,

HAVANNAH HARBOUR, NEW HEBRIDES

Printed at the expense of the Trustees of the Melbourne Public Library.

Melbourne:
Edgerton and Moore, Printers, Flinders Lane East.
1889.

PREFACE.

SHORTLY after arriving in Melbourne a few months ago for the purpose of seeing through the press the translation of the New Testament into Efatese—a work now completed, and, to the honour of Victoria it should be said, as well printed and bound as it could have been in London—I was asked by Professor A. Harper, M.A., on behalf of the Melbourne Public Library, to provide such materials as are now laid before the public in this work. Not anticipating anything of this kind, I had left at Havannah Harbour most of my notes on various New Hebrides languages, and hence could not give, on the present occasion, anything like a comparative grammar of the whole of these languages. But such a work may yet be forthcoming, and the present may be but the prelude to it. While it is true that the New Hebrides languages cannot be properly understood unless we study them in the light of their relationship to the other languages of the Malayo-Polynesian or Oceanic family, it is also true that the languages of the New Hebrides are of great and indispensable importance to the study of Oceanic. The Melbourne Public Library is an institution that is an honour not merely to Victoria, but to Australia. Planted here in this great continent of the Southern Ocean, the Anglo-Saxon race is bound, in the interests of humanity, to complete the investigation of the problems of Oceania so well begun by the illustrious scholars of Europe, who long ago recognised their world-wide importance. Already the Trustees have wisely and worthily taken steps to bring together, from all parts of the world into the Melbourne Public Library, the extant literature relating to these problems.

I deem it a pleasure and an honour to co-operate, in however humble a way, in this truly enlightened movement; and I trust that this little work, though merely introductory and fragmentary, will be found not without real and permanent value. For instance, the late Mr. Gordon, in his notice of the Eromangan dialects (see below, p. 78 and following) has given materials of the highest value to the study of Oceanic, a family of languages spoken by from thirty to fifty millions of the human race. And it need scarcely be said, as it has always been taken for granted by the great scholars above referred to, that the problems of Oceania of deepest interest to mankind can only be solved by the scientific investigation of that linguistic family. In the sketch of the Efatese grammar below it will be noted that various references are made to that family, and I have now merely to refer those who are interested in the subject to the work by the present writer, entitled, "Oceania" (Melbourne and London), published simultaneously with this.

D. MACDONALD.

March, 1889.

SKETCH

OF THE

GRAMMAR

OF THE

EFATESE LANGUAGE.

THE Efatese language is spoken throughout the island of Efate (called by Captain Cook, who discovered it, Sandwich,) and in the neighbouring islets to the north which constitute the Shepherd group, and on a small part of the adjacent coast of Epi. In South-West Bay, Efate, on two small islets called Fila and Meli, and on the east side of the islet of Mai, or Three Hills, in the Shepherd group, the languages or dialects spoken belong to the Maori-Hawaiian branch of the Malayo-Polynesian or Oceanic family, and the people speaking them, or their forefathers within very recent times, have drifted thither in canoes from the Samoan or Tongan groups. The last canoe that drifted to Mai was filled with-people. They had a musket on board, and fought desperately They were nearly all killed, but one is yet living, and portions of the canoe are still preserved. This took place nearly forty years ago. The Efatese language belongs to the Papuan branch of the Oceanic family, as do all the New Hebrides languages, with such trifling exceptions as those mentioned. There are several dialects of Efatese, differing from each other as do provincial dialects of England or Scotland. The Efatese all understand each other when speaking, except the speakers of one dialect. That dialect spoken in the north-eastern part of the Shepherd group is so different from all the rest that those who speak it and those who speak the other dialects do not understand each other. I shall call that the north-eastern dialect. The Efatese is noticed in the work of Gabelentz *(Die Melanesischen Sprachen,)* but his materials were very scanty, consisting of a short list of words obtained from the work of the Rev. Dr. Turner, and a longer and more valuable list furnished by the late Bishop Pattison; the former of a dialect spoken on

EFATESE LANGUAGE. 7

the south of Efate, the latter of the Sesake dialect, spoken on the island of Mai and the neighbouring coast of Epi.

A short grammar of Efatese is given by the Rev. Dr. Codrington in his work on "The Melanesian Languages," who also gives a notice of the Sesake dialect. The former he drew from a translation of the Gospel of Luke by the present writer. All these writers laboured under the disadvantage of not knowing the Efatese Bishop Pattison was a distinguished linguist and his material on the Sesake dialect valuable. The sketch of Gabelentz carefully founded on that material, is by far the most valuable of the above notices of the Sesake dialect, while that of Dr. Codrington is by far the most valuable on the Efatese as spoken in Efate. The whole of the New Testament has been translated into Efatese, the translation being the joint work of the Rev. J. W. Mackenzie, who is stationed on the south side of the island, and myself stationed on the north side in Havannah Harbour. There is a difference of dialect between the south and north side, besides differences at intermediate places; in fact there are slight dialectical differences in almost every village. But as all the people understand each other when speaking, Mr. Mackenzie and I thought it possible to make a kind of compromise literary dialect for the whole of the people so understanding each other when speaking; and most desirable, not only as lessening the expense of printing the Scriptures, but also as a means of uniting the people together, and so helping, in accordance with the spirit of Christianity, to put an end to the separation of tribe from tribe that had been so large a feature of, and so fruitful a source of evil in, the heathen state, and to make it impossible for the future. This work, though not without difficulty, has been accomplished, and the printing of the Efatese New Testament in Melbourne is now just being completed. In carrying on this translation one of our principles was always to use the Efatese just as used by the people, and while using an expression common in one dialect rather than the equivalent expression common in another dialect, to be guided in the choice by a due regard to the interests of the whole people, and keeping in view future generations as well as the present.

EFATESE LANGUAGE.

In the present work I shall give the grammar of the Efatese as spoken in Havannah Harbour, noticing the peculiarities of the other dialects so as to present as completely and intelligibly as possible the phenomena of the language.

ALPHABET AND LETTER CHANGES.

THE vowels are *a, e, i, o, u,* and have the Italian sounds.

The consonants used in the New Testament are *b, f, g, k, l, m, n, r, s, t,* and *p;* of these, *b* stands for both *b* and *p, f* for both *f* and *v, g* for *ng* (as in "sing,") and *p* for *pw* or *kw;* the rest as in English, though *k* may be regarded as for *k* and hard *g* (as in "get,") *s* for *s* and *z,* and *t* for *t* and *d.* The sounds of *d,* hard *g,* and *z* are rare in Efatese, though in some dialects *d* is frequently pronounced with *n,* as *nd,* and hard *g* is heard after *ng,* as N.E. dialect, keigkami (for *keigami*) "we," pronounced *keing—gami.* The common Efatese *t* is often pronounced *ts* in an inland dialect.

LETTER CHANGES.—The most remarkable

changes in Efatese now prevailing are those between *k* and *g* (*i.e.*, *ng*) or *vice versa*, *n* and *g*, *n* (through *g*) and *k*, *b* and *f* or *f* and *b*, *b* or *f* (through *w*) to a mere vowel. It may be remarked that the sounds of *w* and *y* are both heard in Efatese; but we have judged it unnecessary to print these letters and use instead of *w*, *u*, and instead of *y*, *i*, thus *wa* is written *ua*, and *yo*, *io*. Examples of consonant changes :—*gu*, *k* (for *ku*,) "my;" *kinami*, *kigami*, *keigkami*, *nigami*, "we;" *guruni*, *kuruni*, "woman;" *kuru*, *guru*, "gather together;" *ran*, *rag*, *rak*, "time;" also *lag* and *nag* (*l*, *n*, and *r* being interchanged, as well as *n*, *g*, *k* ;) *koro*, *goro*, "enclose," &c. ; *ni*, *gi*, *ki*, "to," "of" (preposition.)

B and *f* are changed constantly, and often the one or the other is used according to the caprice of the speaker, or as to his idea of euphony, as *ba fati*, "do," *i bati*, "he does," *nafatien*, "the doing," *ru brig*, "they do," *nafrigien*, "the doing," *ba fan*, "go thou," *ko ban*, "go ye," *nafanoen*, "the going." *B* and *p* (Efatese *p*) are interchanged also as *pila*, "big," reduplicated *bipila*, "big," and both *b* and *p* are changed with *w* or a vowel as *botai*, or *potai*, "to divide," also *uotai*, *maota*, "divided," reduplicated *b*—or *potauota*; *borai* or *porai*, "rend asunder," *maora*, "rent asunder," reduplicated *porauora*, and *porōra*; *pora*, "to produce," "to spring up or grow," *uora*, "offspring."

In comparing the different dialects various changes are seen besides these as of *m* to *g*; *sumi*, *sugi*, "kiss;" *s* to *n*, *naisuma*, *nainuma*; "a piece of ground partly prepared for a plantation;" *m*, *b*, *f*, *u*, *baram*, *barab*, *baraf*, *barau*, "long," *namoñam*, *namonau*, "grass," *bi*, *mi*, "is," "are," *kabu*, *koau*, Efatese "bread or cakes," *bo*, *mo*, *fo*, *o*, "sign of the future;" *s* to *h* as *latesa*, *lateha*, "six," *se*, *he*, "who?" and many others.

Vowel changes are frequent. What is pronounced *a* in one dialect is pronounced *e* in another, as *safa*, *sefa*, "what?" *namatian*, *namatien*, "the dying," "death;" *i* and *e* may be written the one or the other, according to choice; thus the word "die" may be written *mate* or *mati*; *u* and *o*, as *bonoti*, *bunuti*, "to close" (the one of these is as correct as the other.) On looking at different dialects, we find *ru*, *ri*, "they;" *ku*, *ki*, "you;" *ta*, *sa*, *tu*, *ti*, "not." The terminal vowel of a word in one dialect we find usually omitted in another, as *sifi nakasu, sef nakas,* " what tree or wood ?"

Omission of consonants is not very common ; the last word is sometimes pronounced *kau* for *kasu,* and *asu, aso* and even *so* in different dialects, or rather in different villages ; in N.E. dialect *kai.* At the village close to which the mission house is built in Havannah Harbour, it is *kasu,* and rarely *asu* or *aso ;* at a village a mile distant it is *kau.*

Transposition is rare, as *bunul, bulun,* " to cleanse ;" *silifi, sifili,* " to enter," with transitive preposition *silifi ki, sifili ki,* " to put inside," " enter " (transitive,) " a thing."

When we find a word in many different dialectical forms as *tika, nika, rika, tsika, tsia,* " is not," " no ;" and *nova, noa, no, ti,* " tell," " declare ;" the question as to which form is the most incorrupt is one not to be answered without a due comparison of the Efatese language with the cognate languages. This does not fall within the scope of the present work.

THE ARTICLE.

THE article in Efatese is *n* with vowel before or after, the vowel being usually *i* (or *e,*) but often *a*, as *na kasu*, "tree," "wood;" *in tas, nitas,* or *na tas*, "the sea;" *na famien*, "the eating," "a meal," "food," from *fami*, "to eat." The article is written or printed joined on to the noun in the New Testament. The same article is general in the New Hebrides, and appears in Malagasy as *ny* or *ni*. In Samoan it has the form *le*, east side Mai *re*; Maori, *te;* Meli, *ta* and *t'*. In Efatese the article sometimes appears without the consonant, as *asuma, esuma,* or *nasuma*, "house," (*suma*.) Either *in, ni,* or *na* may be used, often according to the caprice of the speaker. Sometimes the initial consonant of a word has disappeared before the article constantly used prefixed to it, as *nai*, "water;" dialects, *noai*, and *nirai*. A European asking an Efatese the word for "water" and getting *nai* would naturally think the *n* a part of the word; so *naika*, "fish" (Meli *taika*,) is scarcely ever heard without the article *na;* this is true of many other words. It is only in this fossilised way that this common or universal article now exists in Malay. The article, through letter change, assumes various forms; thus, the *e*, which Gabelentz has noticed, of *ekopu*, "house," "inside of house," is the article, though it is pronounced like the short form (*i* or *e*) of the third personal pronoun singular. Dr. Codrington is in error in calling this *e* (or *i*) the "locative," and translating *e fate* (Efate) "at Fate:" Efate is simply the name of the island, *e* being a form of the article as in *Emai* (*Mai*,) and *Emau* (*Mau*.) So in *Aneityum*, *an* is the article. The article *na* in *nagusu*, "nose," appears as *la* in the same word in another village *la usu* (for *la gusu*) "nose." The article also appears as *ng*, and *k*, *n* being readily changed to *ng*, and *ny* to *k*. These different forms of the article are found in the Oceanic generally, as well as in Efatese.

What Dr. Codrington calls the "Personal Article" is either the pronoun of the 3rd person alone, or combined with the prefixed article.

THE PERSONAL PRONOUNS.

THE separate pronouns have the fullest forms and are—

EFATESE LANGUAGE.

North-East dialect.

3rd singular	*nai*	*kinini*		he, she, it
2nd ,,	*nago*	*keina, keiga*		thou (you)
1st ,,	*kinau*	*keino*		I
3rd plural	*nara*	*kiniara*		they
2nd ,,	*kumu*	*kami*		you
1st ,,	*kinami*	*keigema*		we

The verbal pronouns have shorter forms and are—

3rd singular	*i*	*i*		he, she, it
2nd ,,	*ku*	*ko*		thou (you)
1st ,,	*a*	*ni*		I
3rd plural	*ru*	*ri*		they
2nd ,,	*ku*	*ki*		you
1st ,,	*au*	*pu*		we

The nominal suffixes are—

3rd singular	*na*	*na*		his, her, its
2nd ,,	*ma*	*ma*		thy (your)
1st ,,	*gu*	*ga*		my
3rd plural	*ra*	*niara*		their
2nd ,,	*mu*	*mia*		your
1st ,,	*nami* or *gami*	*gemi*		our

The verbal suffixes are—

3rd singular	*ia, ea, na, nia, s, sa*		him, her, it
2nd ,,	*ko*	*ke*	thee (you)
1st ,,	*nau, au*	*o, au*	me
3rd plural	*ra, ta*	*inira*	them
2nd ,,	*mu*	*kama*	you
1st ,,	*gami, nami, gema*		us

The inclusive is, separate—

nigita	*keigite*	I and you

Verbal—

tu	*ti*	I and you

Nominal suffix—

gita	*gite*	mine and yours

Verbal suffix—

gita	*gite*	me and you

The dual of the verbal pronoun is

3rd person	*ra*	*ria*	they two
2nd ,,	*ko ra, ko ro* or *ku rua*	*kia*	you two
1st ,,	*ara*	*moa*	we two

Inclusive—

ta	*ta*	I and you two

These assume the following forms in various Efatese dialects :—

EFATESE LANGUAGE. 17

I, *kinu, anu, enu*; my, *k* (or *ku*,) *g* (for *gu.*)
We, *kamam, komam, kimam, nigami, kigami, igam* or *agam,* and *nigkam* (for *nigam*;) our, *nami, gami, ngkam, kam, mam.*
Thou, *ang, ango, nigo;* thy (your) *m;* thee (you,) *k, ma.*
You, *nikam, akam, akamus, kimu, nimu, nem* or *něĕm, egū;* your, *gu.*
He, *inia, enea, gā, nigā;* verbal pronoun, *ki;* his, *n*; him, *n, s, i, ni,* and it is sometimes absorbed in the final vowel of the verb, merely lengthening it, as *i, e, a, o* or *u.*
They, *enera, inira, nigara;* verbal pronouns, *eru, ĕu, ĭu, u;* their, *r;* them, *r, nira.*
Inclusive, *nigit, nikit, akit, igira, niginda;* nominal suffix, *git, kit.*

The original forms of the Efatese personal pronouns were—

    I, *naku*   We, *nami*
    Thou, *anka*   You, *ankamu*
    He, *i* or *ia*   They, *ĭū,* or *ĕū* or *ū,*

or *ira* or *ara;* inclusive, *nita* I thou : *nami* became changed to *gami, kami,* Malay, *kami,* Malagasy, *ahay;* and *nita* to *gita, kita,* Malay, *kita.* Malagasy, *ika,* Samoan, *ta; naku* became *nau* and *au*, Malay, *aku*, Malagasy, *ahu*, Samoan, *a'u;* and *anka, ankamu, ag* and *akam*, Malay, *ang, kamu*. It does not belong to our present subject to pursue this further. The pronouns, though they are admittedly identical, assume the most extraordinary variety of forms in the various dialects of the Oceanic family.

The separate or emphatic possessive. In addition to the above possessives suffixed to nouns, another possessive is formed suffixed to particles which are either the article, or a preposition or both combined. Thus in Efatese with preposition *ka*, to,—*kagu, kama, kana, kagami* or *kanami, kamu, kara,* "to me," "pertaining to me," "mine," &c., and the same with article, as *a* or *e, kiagu* or *kiegu, kiama* or *kiema*, with a slightly different shade of meaning When the article, as *ana*, is prefixed to *kagu*. &c., the *k* is changed to *g*, as *anagagu, anagama,* "the or what to me," "pertaining to me," &c.; so when the article is abbreviated to *a*, as *agagu, agama, agana, aggami, agamu, agara*. This preposition also appears in the following common forms of the emphatic possessive — *aginau, aginago, aginai, aginami,* agumu, aginara, literally a, "the ;" gi, "to" or "of ;" nau, "me," &c.; and also with n instead of g—anau, anago, anena, anigami, animu, anara, (aneara, aneta, areara, ateta,) &c. In one dialect the article and preposition appear combined as nig, " of the," as nignu, nigag, nigā, nigmam, nigamus, nigara, and in that dialect this is the common form of the sign of the genitive, as nig natamole "of man ;" this in our dialect is ni natamole, gi natamole, or ki natamole, ni, gi, and ki, being all the same preposition. Thus we can say ani se, agi se, or aki se, ' the of whom," " whose ?"- or ani, or agi, or aki John, or without the article ni, or gi, or ki John, "John's." It may be remarked also that this a is used alone with the suffixed pronouns as follows—agu, ama, ana, anami, amu, ara, "the or that which (of) me, mine, thine, his, &c." In Samoan only the emphatic possessive is used ; in Malagasy the nominal suffix is used, and the emphatic possessive also.

CONJUGATION OF THE VERB.

The person and number of the verb are denoted by the above verbal pronouns, thus :—

ba to go, Singular—1. a ba   I go.
                      2. ku ba   thou goest.
                      3. i ba   he goes.
         Plural—1. au ba   we go.
                    2. ku ba   you go.
                    3. ru ba   they go.
          Dual—1. ara ba   we two'go.
                  2. kŏ ro ba you two go.
                  3. ra ba   they two go.

TENSES.—The foregoing is not always equivalent to our present tense thus, *i ba*, while sometimes meaning "he is going," or "he goes," sometimes cannot be thus rendered, as *i ba nanu* (*nanu* "yesterday") cannot be rendered "he goes yesterday," but "he went yesterday."

A kind of past tense is denoted by *ka* between the verbal pronoun and the verb thus—

    Singular—1. a ka ba.
                2. ku ka ba.
                3. i ka ba.
      Plural—1. au ka ba.
              2. ku ka ba.
              3. ru ka ba, they went.

EFATESE LANGUAGE

In one dialect instead of *ru ka ba* they say *ru kui ba*. In some dialects this particle is not used to form this tense.

A kind of past perfect is formed by suffixing *i* (or *e*) to this *ka*, as—

    Sing.—1. a kai ba—I had gone.
           2. ku kai ba.
           3. i kai ba.
    Pl.—1. au kai ba.
           2. ku kai ba.
           3. ru kai ba.

A kind of continuous tense is formed by *bo*, as—

    Sing.—1. a bo ba—I am going.
           2. ku bo ba.
           3. i bo ba.
    Pl.—1. au bo ba.
           2. ku bo ba.
           3. ru bo ba.

This *bo* is also used thus—*i bisa bo tili*, he spake, saying; *i tulena bo ba*, "he arose, going," the going continuing on from his arising.

The future tense is formed thus—

    Sing.—1. a ga uo ba.—I will or shall go.
           2. ku ga uo ba.
           3. i ga uo ba.

Pl.—1. au ga uo ba.
   2. ku ga uo ba.
   3. ru ga uo ba.

This *uo* in one dialect is pronounced *bo* (in others *mo, fo, o,*) and is identical with the *bo* of the continuous tense. The *ga* has the force of a final conjunction "that," "in order to," "to," as *i ga uo ba,* "he to be going."

This *ga* alone forms a kind of imperative or permissive and infinitive, thus—

Sing.—1. a ga ba—that I go, I may or should go.
   2. ku ga ba—you may or should go, go.
   3. i ga ba—he may go, let him go, that he go.
Pl.—1. au ga ba—we to go.
   2. ku ga ba—you to go.
   3. ru ga ba—they to go.

Thus, "he desires you to go," is expressed by *i mesau na ku ga ba,* "he desires it you to go," or "that you go," and "he says you are to go" by *i tili ku ga ba*—"he says you to go," or "that you go." In one dialect this *ga* appears as *k'*, and the verbal pronoun is put between it and the verb, thus,

Sing. 1. *ka ba*, *k'* that, *a* I, *ba* go.
3. *ke ba*, *k'* that, *e* he, *ba* go.

This explains the imperative second person. singular and plural—

ba fa, go thou.

ko ba, go ye, that is,

b', "that;" *a*, "thou;" *fa*, "go;" and *k*, that;" *o*, "you;" *ba*, "go:" the *a* of *ba*, and the *o* of *ko* being fragments of the pronoun second person singular and plural respectively. In the north east dialect the final conjunction *ba* is used in the future tense, instead of *ga*.

THE VERBAL NOUN.

This is formed by suffixing *en* or *an* (pronounced also *ena* or *ana*,) to the verb, thus, *fami*, "eat;" *famien*, "eating," "food;" with article *nafamien*, "eating," "act of eating," "food." This verbal noun may be used in a passive sense as an adjective, thus—*nafinaga famien*, "food for eating," or "eatable." Also one can say *nafamien ni nafinaga*, "the eating of food," or *nafami nafinagan*, "the eating of food." In the latter expression the two words are in the construct state, and to them as if one word (as they are really one compound word) the verbal noun formative particle is suffixed. This formative particle also makes abstract nouns from adjectives as *kasua*, "strong," *nakasuān*, "the being strong," "strength," *uia*, "good," *nauiān*, "the being good," "goodness." All adjectives may be conjugated as verbs, thus—*a uia, ku uia, i uia*, "I am," "thou art," "he is good;" and so in all the tenses In fact, the Efatese verb is a verbal substantive, or verbal adjective, thus —*i ba* is not "he goes," or "he went," but "he (is, or was) going," and *i uia* "he (is, or was) good," and *nauian* is "the state of being good," *nafaan* "the act of going."

The *nomen agentis* is expressed thus—*bokati*, "to strike;" *tea bokati*, "a striker," "a person" or "a thing," as a hammer, "that strikes;" so universally. *Tea* has the force of a relative pronoun, and may best be translated by "what" or 'that," as meaning both "he who," "those who," or "that which," or "the things which," thus—*tea bokati*, "that" or "which strikes." *Tea* is used also with adjectives, as *tea uia*, "that good," "a thing" or "person good." *Te* is also used as an indefinite article, as *te nata*, "any person" or "whatever person." *Te* may

EFATESE LANGUAGE.

also denote "some," as *te ru ban, te ru tok*, "some go, some remain." The article can be prefixed to *te*, as *nete* or *netea*, "something," "anything." Probably *tea* consists of *t'*, a form of the article, and the demonstrative *e* or *ea*, "this" or "that," the combination forming a relative pronoun. Like the English "that" it is sometimes used as a conjunction, signifying "that" or "because" as *i mesauna tiga (te iga) fan*, "he desires that he go;" *i rogtesa nanina te (te i) mate*, "he is afflicted or suffering because his son is dead."

FORMS OF THE VERB.

THE causative is sometimes formed by prefixing *baka* or *faka*, as *mauri*, "live;" *bakamauri*, "preserve alive," "save;" *bura*, full;" *bakafura*, "to fill." The real causative prefix is *ba* or *fa*; the *ka* of *baka* is really a form of the article, as we learn from other Oceanic dialects. *Ba* is sometimes used without the *ka*, as *gani*, "to eat;" *bagani*, "feed;" *bausi*, "to question" (*usi*, "to follow in the track of.") The causative is formed sometimes by *se* (*sa,*) *si*, as *gara*, "strong;" *sigiri*, "to strengthen;"

and with article as *ra* (found also in other Oceanic dialects) *sera*, as *lesoko*, "true;" *seralesoko*, "to deem true," "believe;" *tepalo*, "worthless;" *seratepalo*, "deem worthless," "despise."

The reflexive or reciprocal is formed by *bi*, or *fi*, as *meri*, "do;" *fimeri*, "keep on doing;" *atu*, "smite;" *fiatu*, "smiting each other," "fighting;" *liliu*, "return;" *biliu*, "go backwards and forwards between two places or parties;" *tili*, "to say," "tell;" *fitili*, "back-biting;" *kat*, "to bite;" *fikat* or *fikit*, "given to biting," "savage." It is sometimes merely intransitive, neither the reflexive nor reciprocal force being plain, as *kat*, "bite" (transitive;) *fikat*, "bite" (intransitive.)

A number of adjectives occur with the prefix *ma*, as *kot*, "to break;" *makot*, "broken;" *bora*, "to rend;" *ma(u)ora*, "rent." These are not true passives but reflexives used in a kind of passive sense; such words as *makot, ma(u)ora*, can only be understood by a comparison of other Oceanic dialects, as is the case with many other phenomena of the Efatese language.

A number of adjectives of the same kind as those just noticed are formed by the prefix *ta*, as *fulus*, "to turn round;" *tafulus*, "turned round;" *fifi*, "to involve;" *tafifi*, "involved," *lubaki*, "to pour out;" *talubaki* (also *malubaki*) "poured out." Neither *malubaki* nor *talubaki* is a true passive, thus *noai i malubaki* or *i talubaki* does not mean "the water is poured out" (by some one,) but "the water pours itself out," or "is spilt." There is no true passive in Efatese. And it is only a limited number of words that can take the prefixes noticed. Some words occur with a prefixed form particle, and never without it in Efatese, though without it in some cognate dialect, as *mataku*, "to be afraid;" *mitiri*, "to write;" Malay *takut, tulis*.

The reflexive prefix *ta* is found attached to the causative prefix *ba*, thus *laga* "to be high," "to raise," *balaga* "to raise," *tabalaga* "raised," "made itself raised."

Many verbs and adjectives may be reduplicated, as *malaga*, *malagalaga* "lifted up," "raised," *mitiri* "to write," "paint," "make figures," *miti-mitiri* "figured" (as printed cloth,) *leba, leba-leba* "large," also *leleba*; *gara, garagara*, also *tagaragara* "strong." The general effect of reduplication in Efatese is intensity.

Two Adjective endings occur in Efatese *ena* or *ina*, and *a*, as *pila*, reduplicated *bipila*, with adjective ending *pilana*, *pilena*, or *pilina*, *bipilina* or *bipilena* "great," "big," *barbaruta* and *barbarutena* "fat;" this ending seems to intensify or denote the more permanent possession of the quality denoted by the adjective in Efatese. The other is seen in the word *lasoa* "to have swollen testicles," from *laso* "the testicles." As usual we find the explanation of these only by examining the cognate languages. As in all Oceanic languages there is no comparative and superlative like the English "better," "best;" they say *uia* "good," *uia bipilena* "very good," or "greatly good," *uia bipilena kasu* "exceedingly good." One way, however, of expressing the superlative idea is by the aid of the numeral "one" *siki* or *sikei* as *sikei uia* "one" or "alone good," that is "incomparably good." This numeral takes the nominal suffixes, which must then be translated as nominatives thus—

Sing.—1. *a sikigu*—I alone ("I my one.")

2. *ku sikima*—thou alone.
3. *i sikina*, or *sikinia*—he alone.
Pl.—1. *au sikigami*—we alone.
2. *ku sikimu*—you alone.
3. *ru sikira*—they alone.

They can say *tea sikei uia*, or *tea sikina*, or *tea sikinia uia*, "a thing alone good," or "incomparably good."

THE GOVERNMENT OF THE VERB.—Many verbs are connected with their object by means of the transitive preposition. This is the same preposition as is noticed above as the sign of the genitive *ni, gi*, or *ki*. After the verb the latter is its usual form. It has very various meanings, and sometimes gives a causative meaning to the verb. Examples, *ti ki nia*, "say to him," dialect *noa ki nia*. A second object is placed thus, *ti ki nia sa*, "say to him it," "tell him it." On the other hand, *bat ia ki fatu*, "make it with a stone;" *bati nasuma ki fatu*, "make a house with stone," or "of stone;" *silif ia*, "enter it;" *silifi natamole*, "enter a man" (as a spirit;) *silifi ki nia*. "enter it," as *silifi ki namae block*, "enter," or "cause to enter, a rope into a block;" *net ia*, "strike it" (with something thrown;) *net ia ki fatu,* "hit it with a stone;" but *neta ki fatu,* "strike with a stone," that is, "throw a stone;" *kili ia,* "dig it," as *kili natano,* "dig the earth;" but *kili ki nia,* "dig for it," that is, "dig it," as *kili ki post natano.* "dig a post into the ground;" *kili natano ki post,* "dig the ground with a post;" *sābŏ,* "ignorant;" *i bi sabō sa,* "he is ignorant of it;" *i sabona ki nia,* "he is ignorant of it:" in *sabona,* the *na* is the adjective termination. The *ki* is sometimes glued on to the word, thus *natamole sabonáki,* "a man ignorant, constantly" or "habitually." This *ki* is *ka* in Fiji, and the double endings *naki,* and the like, are common in Oceanic generally. The *na* appears as *ma* in *tanumaki,* "to cover with earth" (*tano;*) *tania,* "earth it;" *tanum ia,* "earth it" (*i.e.,* "put it in the earth;") *tanuma ki nia,* "earth it," or "cover it with earth." *Tanumi naui,* or *tanumaki naui,* "cover with earth," or "plant in the earth, a yam:" the *ki* is the transitive preposition (Malay *kan*), but what is the *i* in *tanumi,* of which the *m* is the adjective ending? In Efatese, if we had no help from kindred dialects, we should say it is the 3rd personal pronoun, and *tanumi naui* literally "cover it the yam in the earth." As the Oceanic adjective ending, however, is *i* in the other dialects, it may be a question whether this *i* is not the adjective ending. But as this adjective ending, as we know from other sources, is originally this 3rd personal pronoun, it is impossible to say more than that in Oceanic this *i* is sometimes used as the pronoun, sometimes as the adjective ending. In Efatese it is very often the ending of the verb when it is transitive, as a verb is necessarily transitive when it takes this 3rd personal pronoun as its object, as *til ia*, "say it;" *bat ia*, "do it" (thus words are printed in the New Testament); but this *ia* is really a suffix, and grammatically should be written (as it is spoken) *tilia, batia,* dialect *tili, bati,* "say it," "do it." Now when the verb takes any other object it retains this *i*, as *tili nafisan,* "say a word," *bati nauisien,* "do work." *Tili* and *bati* may be regarded as verbal nouns or adjectives, "saying," "doing," "saying a word," "doing a work.' Or, in the other case, we must translate "saying it a word," "doing it a work." *Natamole tili nafisan* is "a man habitually saying words," whose business is speaking; *natamole bati nasuma*, "a man whose business is house-making." In other dialects *i* is sometimes the adjective ending, and the word with it is an adjective, the so-called passive, or the word is transitive when the *i* appears to have the force of a transitive particle. In Malay it always appears in the latter use, thus—*tangis*, "wailing," "weeping;" *tangisi*, transitive; Efate *tangisi*, transitive; Samoan, *tangisia*, adjective with a passive sense, but that can be used as a transitive like Malay and Efate *tangisi*. A comparison of cognate dialects, then, leads to the conclusion that this Efate *i* is the same adjective ending that pervades the Oceanic, and that is originally identical with the 3rd personal pronoun. In the same way the adjective ending *n* in Oceanic sometimes appears as having the force of a transitive particle.

THE NOUN.

The noun whether with or without the article, according to use, is unchanged in the nominative or oblique cases. The cases are determined by prepositions or by position in the sentence. Example.—

Singular—
Nom. *John*, John.
Gen. *Ni, gi,* or *ki John,* of John.
Acc. *John* or *ki John,* John.

Singular—
Nom. *fatu,* a stone.
Gen. *Ni, gi,* or *ki fatu.* of a stone.
Acc. *fatu* or *ki fatu,* a stone.

The genitive is also denoted by the construct state, thus *nauot nafanua,* " lord or chief of the country," *misimis fatu,* " knife of stone," *nasuma fatu,* " house of stone." Those nouns which take the nominal suffix, as *nagisana,* " his name," when followed by a noun instead of by the pronominal suffix are in the construct state, as *nagisa John,* " name of John ;" *nagisa nata,* " name of someone ;" so *natuona,* " his foot or leg ;" *natuo nata,* " foot or leg of a person." Not all nouns take the nominal suffix, some require the separate possessive. Names of parts of the body, as hand, eye, &c., take the suffix, perhaps because they are conceived of as parts of a whole. Such words as *nasuma,* "house;" *fatu,* "stone;" *nakasu,* "tree," do not take it. Thus you cannot say *nasumana,* "his house," but you must say *nasum aginai,* "his house;" literally, "the house which to him."

Some verbs govern a noun directly or without an intervening transitive preposition, and also with a preposition when the meaning may be different, as *neti fatu,* "hit a stone;" *neta ki fatu,* "throw a stone." The preposition *ki* is also instrumental as *taia ki misimis,* "cut it with a knife;" *net ia ki fatu,* "hit it with a stone;" *ki* also governs the dative, as *ti ki nia,* "tell to him."

Case is sometimes determined by position in the sentence without a preposition as *ti ki nia asa,* "say to him it;" *milu isa,* "depart from it;" *i milu natokon asa,* "he departed from the village on account of it;" so we can say *net ia ki fatu,* or *net ia fatu,* "hit it or him with a stone," while *net ia fatu isa* "is hit him with a stone on account of it" (something.)

NUMBER.—The noun is singular or plural without change of form. The singular may be definitely expressed by the numeral "one," as *nata sikei,* "one person," "a person;" *sikei* being also used as the indefinite article. The plural is denoted by *mera uan*, dialects *māga*, *manag*, as *nata mera uan*, *fatu mera uan*, "persons" or "stones." Another way of expressing the singular dual or plural of a noun when in the nominative is by means of the verbal pronoun; thus *nata rū ban*, "men go;" *nata i ban*, "a man goes;" *nata ra ban*, "two men go."

GENDER.—Gender is denoted by the words "man" and "woman" used with other nouns, as *nanui* or *nanoi*, "a husband," "man," "*vir*," *naguruni*, "a wife," "woman," "a female," thus—*to*, "fowl;" *to nanui*, "male fowl," "cock;" *to naguruni*, "female fowl," "hen;" *nanina nanui*, "his son;" *nanina naguruni*, "his daughter." Some words are naturally male or female, as *tema*, "father," *reit*, "mother." The word *nanoi*, or without article *anoi*, in one dialect is *maane* or *moan*, and for the word *guruni* is used in that dialect *fafine*.

Some words can be used according apparently to the choice of the speaker, either with or without the article. Some are always used with the article. In the New Testament the article is printed prefixed to the noun. Sometimes the article, in one form or another, having been constantly used with a noun in an earlier period of the language, is now practically a part of the word, and can only be recognised by those who have an intimate knowledge of the language, or after a comparison of the cognate dialects. This is in accordance with the fact that the Efatese language is an extremely analytic modern dialect of an ancient inflected tongue.

THE NUMERALS.

DIALECTIC FORMS.

1. sikei, ite, sikitik.
2. rua.
3. tolu.
4. bātĕ.
5. lima.
6. latesa, latcha.
7. larua.
8. latolu.
9. lifiti, lovita.
10. rualima, ralima, tualima.
11. rualima sikei temate (or atmate) sikei.
12. rualima sikei temate rua.
13. rualima sikei temate tolu.

20. rualima rua.
21. rualima rua temate sikeï.
22. rualima rua temate rua.
23. rualima rua temate tolu.
30. rualima tolu.
40. rualima bātĕ.
50. rualima lima.
60. rualima latesa.
70. rualima larua.
80. rualima latolu.
90. rualima lifiti.
100. bunti. dialect *tifili*.
200. bunti rua.
300. bunti tolu.
1000. manu. dialect *bon*.
2000. manu rua.
3000. manu tolu.

ORDINALS.—

Dialect (as in New Testament.)

1st.	kiskei.	kasikei.
2nd.	kerua.	karua.
3rd.	ketolu.	katolu.
4th.	kefate.	kafate.
5th.	kelima.	kalima.
6th.	kelatesa.	kalatesa.
7th.	kelarua.	kalarua.

C

		Dialect (as in New Testament.)
8th.	kelatolu.	kalatolu.
9th.	kelifiti.	kalifiti.
10th.	kerualima.	karualima.

For "first" also *be* is sometimes used, *be* being an adjective signifying "preceding" or "first," or a verb signifying "to precede," "go before," or "first."

The causative form, that is, denominative verbs formed from the numerals of the causative form, signifies "to do so many times" as—

bakasikei	to do once.
bakarua	to do twice.
bakatolu	to do thrice.
bakabate	to do four times.
bakalima	to do five times.
bakalatesa	to do six times.
bakalarua	to do seven times.
bakalatolu	to do eight times.
bakalafiti	to do nine times.
bakarualima	to do ten times.
bakabunti	to do a hundred times.
bakamanu	to do a thousand times.

One by one, &c., is thus expressed—

sikisikei   one by one.

rua rua	two by two, in twos.
tolu tolu	three by three, in threes.
bātĕ bātĕ	in fours.
lima lima	in fives.
latesa latesa	in sixes.
larua larua	in sevens.
latolu latolu	in eights.
lifiti lifiti	in nines.
ralima ralima	in tens.

The cardinals and causatives may be made into verbal or abstract nouns; thus, *naralimān*, the being ten, *nafakaralimān*, the doing ten times. The above *temate* or *atmate* has the force of the conjunction "and," as, *rualima rua temate rua*, twenty and two, or twenty together with two.

The numeral "one" is used also as the indefinite article *nata sikei*. "a man," or "a person." It would seem that *sera* is a form of the numeral "one," as in one dialect for *siki tau*, "an only child," we have *tema ser*. The cardinals are sometimes used as substantives and put before the noun, as *ralima natamole i latesa*, "tens of men are six;" or *ralima ni natamole i latesa*, that is, "sixty men." They can be used also as verbs, as *i sikei, i rua, i tolu;* in *i tolu* the *i* must sometimes be translated in a plural sense; "they (are) three," that is, the things are three. If persons are spoken of the plural verbal pronoun must be used, as *ru tolu*, "they (the persons) are three." The cardinals can be used also as adjectives, as *natamole tolu*, "three men."

The numerals from six to ten are combinations of the first five numerals, thus—

latesa is for	*lima tesa,*	five (and) one.
larua	*lima rua,*	five (and) two.
latolu	*lima tolu,*	five (and) three.
lifiti	*lima bati,*	five (and) four.
rualima	two of five,	ten.

The word *rualima* thus formed is treated as a single word, like the English word "ten," and *rualima rua* is two tens, twenty; *rualima lima*, five tens, fifty. For ten thousand can be said *manu rualima,* or *rualima ni manu;* for thirty thousand, *manu rualima tolu*, or *rualima ni manu i tolu.* In some of the New Hebrides Papuan dialects (in Ambrym, Mallicolo and Santo) the numerals from 6 to 9 are thus formed, while the more ancient Oceanic word for "ten" is retained, which in Malagasy,

EFATESE LANGUAGE.

Malay and Samoan is *fulu* (or a form of it;) in others the more ancient Oceanic words for all the numerals from 6 to 10 are retained, and are the same as in Malagasy, Javanese and Samoan, for instance in Santo, in the dialect given in the grammar of that dialect below. In that dialect also it will be noticed that the adjective ending *na* attached to the causative of the numeral makes the ordinal, as *vakarua*, "twice;" *vakaruana*, "second." In the Eromangan (see Grammar) the same adjective ending as *ngi* (for *ni*) attached to the cardinal forms the ordinal, as *duru*, "two;" *durungi*, "second." The Santo *lēl*, 100, given in Mr. Gordon's Grammar is in another Santo dialect *lifili*, which compares with the Efatese *tifili*, 100. On the other hand, his *ruwun*, 1000, in another Santo dialect is *rūna*; *ruwu-n* compares with Malagasy *arivo* (*arivu*,) Malay *ribu*, Java *ewu*, Samoan and Tongan *afe*, 1000.

THE DEMONSTRATIVE PRONOUN.—This, *ua, ne, uane, ua naga, ua netu, netu, se;* dialects, *kis, nis, kistu, nistu, i, uai, situ, ke, nduk, eri, eru.*

That, *uān*, or *uāna, netu*; dialect, *arai.* In all these there are only a few demonstrative particles, of which other combinations besides these are sometimes used.

THE INTERROGATIVE PRONOUNS—*sē* or *sēi*, "who;" dialect, *fē* or *fēi*; the latter is used on the south side of Efate, that is the side facing Eromanga, which is about seventy miles distant.

sefa or *safa, sefana, nasefa, na sefana, nasā, nasāna* (contraction of *nasefana*) "what?" In *nasefa, na* is the article, and *nasefana* is "what there?" In the south dialect, *nafte* is "what?" or *nafite—na* the article, *fi* "what?" and *te* "that or this (thing;)" so *sefa,* or *sifi te,* "what that or this (thing:)" the *s'* is demonstrative.

In the north-east dialect, *kehe* is "who?" (*he* for *se,*) and *nahefe* (for *nasefa*) "what?" also *nefehe* (like *nafite*) "what?" "which?"

Who? (plural) is expressed by *semani,* dialect *semai* or *semei?* In north-east dialect *kehe maga?*

There are only two interrogative pronouns in all these combinations, *é* or *ei* and *fa,* or we may regard *fei, fé,* "who?" as a third.

INDEFINITES.—The interrogative *fa* or *ma*, with the demonstrative *tuna* suffixed to it, as *fatuna* or *matuna*, with article *nɪfatuna* or *namatuna*, denotes " "anything," "something," "somehow ;" and *se*, "some person or persons," as *segamu*, "who of (*ga*) you ?" or "some or any one of you ;" *segara* or *seara*, "some (of them.")

Also *sefa*, &c., is used thus—*natamole sefa*, "a man some or other ;" *fatu sefa*, "a stone whatever." It is difficult to give the exact meaning of the pronoun "what ?" in this latter indefinite use of it. In the same indefinite way *ma* occurs in *mau* (*u* demonstrative) after a verb, before which the negative adverb is used, as *i ti ba mau*, "he not going however, or at all ;" *a ti libis ia mau*, "I did not see it at all." It gives a kind of vague emphasis to the negative sentence, from which, however, it can be omitted, as *a ti libis ia*, "I did not see it," but its use is very common.

The Relative Pronoun. — *Nag*, "who," "that," "which," as *natamole nag i libis ia*, "the man that saw it ;" *nafisan nag i uia*, "the word, or a word that is good." *Uane* can be used for *nag*. The use of *te* as a kind of relative is not so frequent, but *te nag*, or *te uane*, is much used to denote "that" (person or thing,) "who," or "which," as *te nag*, or *te uane i til ia i uia*, "what he says it, is good"—literally, that or "what he says it, is good;" *te nag*, or *te uane ru ban*, "those who go." The oblique cases of the relative (originally demonstrative) are expressed thus: *nafanua nag i milu is* "the land from which he departed," literally "the land that he departed from it;" *natamole nag i ti ki nia asa*, "the man to whom he told it," literally "the man that he told to him it;" *nata nag i libis ia*, "the man whom he saw," literally "the man that or who he saw him." The relative is often omitted.

A peculiar word in Efatese is *tuma*, dialect *ndumbu*, which takes the nominal suffix thus—

a tumagu bat ia	I of my own accord did it.
ku tumama	you of your own accord did it.
i tumana	he of his own accord did it.
au tumagami	we of our own accord did it.
ku tumamu	you of your own accord did it.
ru tumara	they of their own accord did it.

When the pronoun after the verb denotes the same person as the actor, the phrase is used reflexively, as *i tumana libis ia klas*, "he saw himself in a glass;" *ru tumara rum ira*, "they love each other." This word really means "to grow" (Meli, *tubu,*) and *i tumana* is literally "he his growing," or, as it were, spontaneously acting or thinking according to his inner nature. In Meli, *tubu,* "to grow," is also used in the sense of doing spontaneously or of his own accord, or from oneself.

ADVERBS.

Kua or *gua,* "how?" also *kısafa, kasā, kasāna,* "how?" literally "as what?" *kuan, kuanaga,* "how this?" *kite,* as "like." *Sē,* "where?" as *i baki se,* or *i baki safa,* "he goes where?" *i ba se,* or *ba safa,* "he comes from where?" In one dialect *ē* is "where?" and in the northeast dialect it is *mbe,* as *e doko mbe, i toko sā,* or *sē,* "it is where?" "When?" is expressed by *nagasa,* i.e., *naga,* "time;" and *sa,* "what?" dialect, *sefa rag? rag* or *naga* being the article *n'* or *r'* (or *l'* in dialect *lag,*) and *aga* or *ana* (dialect *rān*) "time." "How?" is also expressed by *takan?* and used indefinitely; *takan* signifies "so," "thus." "How many?" is *bīsa?* (dialect *bīa;*) *bisa* is a denominative verb of the reciprocal form, formed from the interrogative

(Malay *barapa*.) *Tabale se, tabali sa*, and *tabale safa*, "like what?" "how?" *tabu*, "like," "to be like;" *le*, "thing;" and *sa*, "what?" "Here," *se, naga, i;* "there," *ban, ana* or *ina, netu*.

The "directives" *mai, banotu*, dialect *baina*, are denominative, or departiculative verbs of the causative form, from the adverbs *i*, "here," *notu* or *otu* and *ina* "there:" thus *mai* literally means "to make for here," "to come" (in the direction of the speaker,) and *banotu* or *baina*, "to make for there," "to go" (in a direction from the speaker,) and *ban*, "to go away," may possibly be a word of the same kind. That these words are denominatives of the causative form is plain from a comparison with the similar words in the Malagasy.

The negative adverb is *ti*, dialects *tu, ta, ndi;* often *ba* is suffixed to *ti*, as *tiba*. This *ba*, though originally a preposition, is used as a verb substantive, and *tiba* denotes "not is," or "is not," and is always used before verbs. When *ka* is suffixed to the negative, as *tika*, dialects *tsika tsia, rika*, it is commonly not used before a verb, but in the sense of "no," or "is not," as *i tika*, "it is not;" *i tika ki nia*, "it is not to him, or in his possession." This *ka*

EFATESE LANGUAGE. 47

is a verb substantive, and probably the same as is used (see above,) as an auxiliary of the indefinite or historical tense. In one dialect the negative *ta* becomes *sa* in the imperative, as *i ta ban*, "he did not go," but *ba su ban*, "go not."

"Yes" is expressed by *io*; dialect, *ōrĭ*; *uis* and *ui* are also used.

"To-day" is expressed by *maisa*; dialect, *mēs*, the *s* or *sa* denoting "this."

"To-morrow," *mitimei*; dialect, *matol*.

"Day after to-morrow," *wāsa, āsa*.

"Third day," *bog tolu*, or *moga tolu*.

"Fourth day," *bog* or *moga bate*.

"Fifth day," *bog* or *moga lima*

"Yesterday," *nanu*; dialects, *nanum, nanofa*.

"Day before yesterday," *nano asa*.

Third, fourth, fifth day, as before.

PREPOSITIONS.

THE Efatese language is highly syntactical. As the cases are often denoted by the position of words in the sentence, prepositions are few. The most used is the one already familiar *ni, gi*, or *ki*. In the form of *ni, gi*, or *ki*, it is the sign of the genitive (which, however, is sometimes expressed by the construct state.) As a transitive preposition it usually has the form of *ki,* and that form is also used in the instrumental sense "by" or "with."

Bai or *bei,* "in" or "on" (Fiji *vei,*) occurs as *i lek bei a,* "he looks on it." *Ni* in one dialect combines with the article and appears as *nig. Nig* denotes "of," as *nig nata,* "of" or "belonging to a man;" and also "for," as *i nig natamole mate,* "he died for men." In other dialects this is expressed by *ma, magi,* or *mini,* as *i masa mer ia,* "he for him did it;" *i magi natamole mate,* "he for men died;" *i mini au mer ia,* "he for me did it." The *ma* is the same preposition which appears as *ba* in *bai,* and the *gi* or *ni* is suffixed to it. This preposition as *bi* or *bai,* dialect *mi,* is very much used as a kind of verb substantive, as *i bi natamole,* "it is a man;" *i bi,* or *i bai lesoko,* "it is true," literally, "a true thing"—*le* "thing," and *soko* "true." But this word *bai* or *bi* is never used thus, except immediately before a noun—thus one could not say for "it is" *i bi*. This is because the word is not originally a verb substantive but the preposition, or (*bai*) the preposition combined with the pronoun of the third person. As already noticed. this preposition as a verb substantive in the sense defined is also much used, suffixed to the negative in *tiba;* accordingly *tiba* is not equivalent to *tika.* One can say *namatakuan i tika,* " fear is not," " does not exist," " there is no fear ; " but not *namatakuan i tiba.* As *bi* can only be used before a noun, so *tiba* only before a verb.

Ma or *me* denotes " with," " together with."

Sometimes a verb, or a verb combined with a preposition, is used for a preposition. Perhaps *baki,* " to," is of this kind, as *i bisa baki nata,* " he spoke *unto* a man ; " *ba* " to go," and *ki* " to." Thus, *i baki se ?* " he goes where ? " *i baki suma,* " he goes to the house." The above *lek bai;* dialect, *libi,* " to look on or upon," " to see ; " is also used thus, *i ban libi nata,* " he goes to a man," literally " he goes to see a man ; " *i ban libi sia,* " he goes to (see) him."

CONJUNCTIONS.

" AND" is expressed by *go;* dialect, *ne;* also by the preposition *ma* or *me,* literally " with," " together with."

A final conjunction is *ka* or *ga,* " that," " in order to," " to ; " and *ba* (north-eastern dialect.) *Ba* or *b'* is used in all dialects in the 2nd singular imperative, and *k'* in the 2nd plural imperative; *ba fan,* " that thou go "; *ko fan,* " that ye go," "go ; " *ka fan,* " that I go ; " *ke fan,* " that he go," " let him go." A different order is observed in *a ga fan,* " I to go," " that I go ; " *i ga fan,* " he to go," " let him go ; " *ku ga fan,* " you to go," " go."

In one dialect *fe* has an indefinite connective signification " but," &c.

Bo (dialect *kai*) is used to connect verbs, as *i tilia bo ban,* " he said it, then went ; " *i bisa bo tili,* " he answered, saying ; " *i bami bo buka,* " he ate to being filled," or " continually to being filled." This *bo* we have already seen as a sign of the present or continuous tense, and as used to help to express the future tense. It is probably the above preposition *b'* and the third personal pronoun *o,* and *bo,* when used thus before a verb, expresses what is really a kind of infinitive or gerundive ; *kai* (compare *bai*) is similarly to be explained as the preposition *k'* or *ka,* and the pronoun of the third person *i.* It may be remarked that though *i* is the usual vowel of the pronoun of the third person in Oceanic, *o* (or *u*) also sometimes occurs, though more commonly in the demonstrative. In Oceanic the pronoun of the third person is used also in demonstratives.

Kite, dialect *ko*, " or," also used at the end of a sentence interrogatively. Another interrogative particle thus used is *ta*.

Bĕ, dialect *fĕ*, " if ;" also *uān*, " if."

INTERJECTIONS.

" O " USED after nouns is the sign of the vocative, as *temagami O*, " O our father."

uana! " look out ! "

ako! " alas," as *ako tai O*, " alas O brother " (in bewailing the dead ;) *ako ki nu*, " woe is me ;" *ako ri*, and *ako ri la*, " alas now, alas now indeed."

The particle *la* is much used as a kind of indefinite adverb or interjection, as *uis la*, " yes indeed ; " it often cannot be translated.

SYNTAX.

THE structure of the sentence is simple. The adjective follows the noun. The nominative precedes the verb. No verb can be used without the verbal pronoun, thus one could not say *natamole ban*, but *natamole i ban*, "a man goes;" *natamole ru ban*, "men go." Even when the separate pronoun is used, the verbal pronoun must be used along with it, thus, not *nara ban*, but *nara ru ban*, "they go;" on the other hand the verbal pronoun alone with the verb forms a complete sentence, as *ru ban*, "they go;" *i ban*, "he goes;" *a ban*, "I go;" *au ban*, "we go;" *ku ban*, "you go." The object follows the verb as *i libi natamole*, "he sees men." The following, taken from the translation of the New Testament, may be given as a specimen of the language :—

2 Timothy, II. 14-23.

14 Ba fati ra ruga miroa berakati tea mau uane, bo bisa suki ra narai Nauot nag ruga ti toko bilea mole ki nafisan, bati sa ki te
15 uane ru to rogo. Ba toko meri sera rogo kuga uia narai Atua, kuga bi tea uisiuis tika namalierien bo toko potai mitaki nafisan
16 nag i bi lesoko. Me ba talele ki nafisan palo, iga uo risu baki nafolofolon sa

17 bipilena, go nafisan nigara iga uo bafaga
18 bakauli namanuk poa; Umenaio go Fileto ra bi segara; natamole nag ru atac sapo nalesoko, bo tili nag natulenan i nu su, go
19 ru roa buele ki naseralesokoen ni tete. Me nalakena kasua ni Atua i tu, go namitiri ua naga i toko osa, Nauot i atae te anena ; go, sera natamole nag i so nagie Nauot iga
20 makota ki nafolofolon sa. Te nasuma bipilena las kolet go las silifa i toko osa, me las nakasu go las natano i mero toko osa; go tete i sela tea uia go tete
21 i sela tea sa. Uan te nata iga tumana bilosi bisaki nia ki te uane, iga uo bi las sela tea uia, tabu toko, uia ki Nauot toko, bo toko raki sera nauisien uia iga bat
22 ia. Ba sefa tua ki namesauen sa ni natamole busafusa, me ba koba te uane i lena, naseralesokoen, narumien, intamate me te uane ru toko tafisafisa ki Nauot ki popo
23 uia. Me ba talele ki nafaususien palo me bunufunoi, ku atae a nag i bi nalake nafilean.

The numerals from one to ten in various New Hebrides dialects:—

Epi 1.	Epi 2.	Epi 3.	Epi 4.	Epi 5.
taga	saka	tei	tai	sagkai
lua	lua	lua	tshua	lua
tolu	selu	tolu	tolu	tou
vare	veri	vate	beri	bas
lima	lima	lima	tshimo	lima
orai	oraka	ari	ari	loktagkai
olua	olua	alua	alua	lokua
orolu	orolu	arolu	arolu	lokutou
wovare	averi	kiveri	koveri	lokubas
loelima	lualima	loelima	ruelima	luanma

Ambrym 1.	Ambrym 2.	Ambrym 3.	Ambrym 4.
hu	hu	hu	sua
ru	ru	ru	lo
sul	sul	sul	si
vit	vit	vitu	vier
lim	lim	lim	lim
limsi	livsi	lise	melipsies
liuru	liuru	liuru	melipo
livsul	livsul	lisul	melepsi
laifiet	rafet	lafar	meper
saghul	sag'ul	sagul	sogapi

Paama.	Pentecost.	Oba.
tas	tual	katea
elua	elu	karua

EFATESE LANGUAGE.

PAAMA.	PENTECOST.	OBA.
etelu	etol	katolu
ehat	epiet	kabate
elima	elim	kalima
ahitai	lowal	kaono
aulua	liplu	kambitu
autel	liptol	kabwalu
auhat	lapat	kahibwa
haluelima	siamnoh	hagafulu

MALLICOLO 1.	MALLI. 2.	MALLI. 3.	MALLI. 4.
etea	soka	bokol	sikei
erua	eru	nrua	eru
etolu	etir	ndila	erei
efata	ebit	mbis	evats
elima	elim	elima	erim
eono	aroptis	robokol	sukai
ambitu	robru	rokorua	wiu
oalu	arobtir	roktil	woroi
ehive	aripi	rohobis	obats
hagafulu	sagafur	sagaful	sigab

SANTO 1.	SANTO 2.	SANTO 3.	SANTO 4.	SANTO 5.
tewa	tea	mokes	tea	tewa
rua	rua	morua	rua	rua
tolu	tolu	morolu	tolu	tolu

56 GRAMMAR OF THE

Santo 1.	Santo 2.	Santo 3.	Santo 4.	Santo 5.
fate	bate	motar	fate	va
lima	lima	molima	lima	lima
oan	merav	kakes	arafi	ono
vitu	raverua	kafakarua	raferua	vitu
al	ravitu	kafakarolu	rafitou	alu
siwa	torobat	kafakatar	rabat	tshiwa
sanafuru	ulátea	sinafulu	sa'bulu	sinafulu

Tana 1.

kadi
kaiyu
kesel
kuvet
karilum
karilum kadi
karilum kaiyu
karilum kesel
karilum kuvet
karilum karilum

EFATESE LANGUAGE.

The Personal Pronouns in some of the New Hebrides Dialects.

	I.	THOU.	HE.	WE.	YOU.	THEY.
Santo—	nau	niko	nai	anam	amiu	ratua
Verb. pro.—ka		ko	mo			ta
Mallicolo 1—kena		kuno	agei	kamam	kam	kara
Verb. pro.—na		ko	ti	ko	ki	riti
Mallicolo 2—inau		aigka	ne	namite	amite	arar
Verb. pro.—ni		ke	ni	neti	khate	ti
Ambrym— ni		nig	ge	kima	kimi	nyere
Verb. pro.—na		o	ĩ	mâ	mi	ī
Paama— inau		keiko	kei	komei	kami	keila
Verb. pro.—na		ki	e	mo, me,	mi	u, ī
Epi 1— nagku		aiko	gana	amai	amun	gā
Verb. pro.—ni		ku	ti	me	ke	le
Epi 2— kinu		tau	tarani	komam	kam	nala
Verb. pro.—ni		ka	i	u	ko	li
Epi 3— kinyu		tshau	nai	komim	kam	nala
Verb. pro.—na		ko	ri	ni	ku	ah

PREFACE.

THE following sketches of the grammar of the Eromangan language and of a language or dialect spoken on the west side of the island of Espiritu Santo, the most northern and largest of the New Hebrides group, are the work of the late Rev. J. D. Gordon. Mr. Gordon had in the noblest Christian spirit come out to Eromanga all the way from Canada, to take the place of his brother who had fallen a martyr to the fury and the misconception of the savages of that island, as had John Williams before him. Mr. J. D. Gordon lived and laboured for some years on that island. He was a large hearted man and did not confine his efforts to Eromanga alone. Some stray natives of Santo having been thrown upon his charity, he endeavoured to learn their language, and afterwards went to their home with them on Santo, and spent nearly a year there learning the language of that place and doing the work of a missionary among the people. He then returned to

Eromanga where he fell a martyr about the beginning of 1872. The two following sketches had been written shortly before his death and also the Santo vocabulary. I give the sketches as he left them, though had he prepared them for publication, doubtless he would have put them in a somewhat different and fuller form. To the Santo vocabulary I have added the corresponding or equivalent Efatese words. I have not taken the liberty to alter in any essential matter what Mr. Gordon has left. It should be observed that he used (and I have left unaltered) *i* for *ai*, *x* for *au*, *c* for *oi*, and *z* for *sh*. He had the two grammars written in parallel columns, and not as in the following pages separately.

My friend, the Rev. H. A. Robertson, who succeeded Mr. Gordon on Eromanga, lent me the original manuscript, from which I made a few years ago the copy now given to the public. A notice of the Eromangan will be found in the work of Gabelentz. It was drawn up mainly from materials furnished by the first Mr. Gordon (the Rev. G. N. Gordon.) There is also a brief notice of some Santo dialect in the work of the Rev. Dr. Codrington.

SKETCH

OF THE

EROMANGAN GRAMMAR.

ARTICLE.

n, if any; inseparable, as neteme, man; nasiven, woman.

si, one; *si neteme*, one, or a man; *neteme mori*, the man, that person spoken of or referred to—definite.

The article *n* disappears in the plural, thus:—
oveteme, men.
ovasiven, women.
itnatemen, male.
itovatimen, males.
itnasiven, female.
itovasiven, females.
nokoben nugko im nugkon, both hands.
nimtum, eye (your.)
sumpat nimtum nugko im nugkon, shut both your eyes.

NOUN.

Genders, two only :—
itnateman, male.
itnasiven, female.
nalx itnateman, a male child.
itemen, father (his.)
dineme, mother.
nate, Father, abba.
name, mother.
avensi, brother (his,) or sister, one woman speaking of another; *veven*, sister, applied by males to females; natemonok, a chief; nasimnalam, female chief, chief's wife.

The personal pronouns are of common gender :—
Iyi, he or she.

NUMBER.—This is indicated by the prefix *ov*, *ōvun*, and the suffix *sū*, *omwi sū*, as,
lo sū, canoes, &c.
lo su lo su, all the canoes.
nalx, a child.
ovalalx, children.
oveteme su, all men.
oveteme omwisū, none left.
dōmō, a stranger.

EROMANGAN LANGUAGE.

ovun domo, strangers.
kos sū, we all (together.)
kos en duru, we two.
lo en duru, two ships.

In the formation of some words, *ra* is prefixed, and *me* suffixed, in the plural, thus:—

avñg, my friend.
ravūgeme, my friends.

CASE.—This is marked by the possessive pronoun following, and by a particle prefixed, as:—

nokobug, my hand.
nokopmū, or *mi,* thy hand.
nokoben, his hand.
nokobent, our hands (Inclusive.)
nokopmam, our hands.
nokepmi, your hands.
nokobenda, their hands.
nokop 'mu, pl., yours.
nitug, my son, or child.
nitum, thy child.
nitni, his, or *netni.*
nitnint, child of us two.
nitnin teme, children, &c.
nitnemam, ch. of us two (Ex.)
niteme, your (two) child.

ovun iteme, children, &c.
nitindi, of them two.
nitin dime, pl., two.
or *nitin deme,* plural.
nitumo, thy (sing.) children.
ovum nitumo, the same.
avug, my friend ; *avugsi,* my brother.
apmi, thy; *apmi si,* thy brother.
aven, ravug si eme,
avent, rapmi si eme, thy brethren.
apmam, rapmam si eme.
ravineme.
ravug eme, my friends.
rumokeponeme, grandchildren
rumokepondeme, grand children of more than one, as of Abraham, Isaac, and Jacob.
nimo enyx, my house.
lō eni, or *isen,* his canoe.
nuru enug kam, our place.
itemen enug kos, our father (Incl.)

The dative and accusative cases are marked by separable and inseparable particles, as :—

(1.) Dative—
    po yx, to me.
    pug kik, to thee.
    pugi, to him.

EROMANGAN LANGUAGE.

pun ora, to them.
pug kūm, to you.
punok, to thee.

(2.) Accusative—
irag, unto or against me.
iram, thee.
iran, him, &c,
irant, iramam,
irami, iranda unto or against them.
tovun-e-yx, for me.
tovunok, tovuni,
tovun-e-kos,-kam,
tovun-e-kūm, for you.
tovun-ora, for, on account of them.
ukili tovun-e-yx, learn of me.
umnakī ugi, to wish, or *like.*
umnaki-wok-o-yx.
    -wug kik,-ugi.
    -wug kūm,-wokonda.
nisikog, for me; *-om,* for you; *-on,* for him.
-kont,-komam, -omi, -onda.

ADJECTIVE.

THE adjective follows (usually) the noun, which it qualifies, as—
  netemi aremī, a good man.

neteme momu aremī, a man more good.
neteme aremī wokon, a man good only.
ra nūsian, exceedingly.
aremī indowi, good always, or essentially good.
momu aremī ra yx, or, *irag*, better than I.
irag is preferable to *ra*.
tantop, momu tantop, tante vakepe, tall or high, &c.
virok or *ūrekis, mŏmū virok, novsirian*, small, &c.
wi, a particle, when applied to adjectives, indicates diminution; it is appended to verbs, also, as—
nakan, bitter, hatred.
nakanwi, bitterish, dislike.
ovug kam wi, give us a little.
enugkamwi, abode, home, habitation, local, of the *spot* rather than the *houses*.

NUMERALS.

1, sī.
2, dūrū.
3, desel.
4, devat.
5, sukrim.

EROMANGAN LANGUAGE. 67

6, sukrim mĭsekī.
7, sukrim narū.
8, sukrim desel.
9, sukrim mindevat.
10, narolem.
11, narolem tampogones sī.
20, narolem dūrū.
100, narolem narolem.
mampum, first in order.
ra nōbūm, first in time.
duṙu su, both.
si ugi first, in time.
durugi, second, &c.
sī teven, one only.
sī teven go, one of each.
durugo, two of each, apart, &c.
sī teven go ra narolem go, the first (proportionally) of each ten; a tithe; *lō sukrim moveteme ra mumpon devatugo*, four men in each canoe.

ORDINALS.

sīugi, 1st.
durugi, 2nd.
deselugi, 3rd.
devatugi, 4th.
sukrimugi, 5th. &c.

TIMES.

nimpugon sīteven, once.
nimpugon duru, twice.
nimpugon desel, three times.
nimpugon devat, four times.
nimpugon sukrĭm, five times.
dan sī, some time, to come.
sī en dan, the same.
sī dan, one day.
dan duru, two days.
ra sī dan, in (on) one day.
sī danemindog, last Sabbath.
danemindog sīugi, next Sabbath.
danemindog duru, two Sabbaths ago.

PRONOUNS.

1st. Personal—

yx, I. *kos*, we (Inclusive.)
kik, thou. *kam*, we.
iyi, he. *kimi*, ye.
irora, they.
kos en duru, we two (Inclusive.)
kam en duru, we two.
kim en duru, you two.
iroran duru, they two.

2nd. Possessive, Genitive or Possessive—
enyx, of me, my or mine.
enugkik, of thee, thine.
eni, his.
enugkos, ours (Inclusive.)
enugkam, ours.
enugkimi, yours.
enirora, theirs.

3rd. Relative—
mori is used as a relative.
mori nimpe, the or that particular thing, just there.
pe = it (redundant.)
ran dan su mori, in, or on, the days referred to.
pe su, plural.

4th. Interrogative—
sing., *mē*, who?
pl., *mē-e-mē*, who?
tiē? siē, what?
muntie? musie, what else?
eneme, whose?
itokowo, which?
kimagkūo, what are you thinking about?
kimawo? what are you going about?

E

kūmawo (pl.)
pōwo? how could? suggestive of difficulty, *pōwo pire?*

5th. Demonstrative—
imō, this.
ima, that.
imo sū, these.
ima su, those (unusual.)
ipema, that one.
iyihi, it is right here.
irora mō, these here.
ti tewa, one; *ti tui*, another.
te ti tewai, any one.

6th. Indefinite—
sī ĭm sī, one and another.
sī kū sī, one or another.
duru su, both.
tawi sī, no one.
sī ke sī, one or another (interesting.)
sī ke neteme, thus spoken if there is a desire to see him.
sī momu, another.
sī mori, the one who.
sī en tie sī, anything.
sī ke irora, (as above.)

iyi-e-ko-sī, he alone.
nugkon, a division, some.
nugkondeme, some of them.
tiame su, things, property.

7th. Reflexive—
yx pe yx, I myself.
kik-e-pe-kik, thou thyself.
iyi pe iyi, he himself.
irora pe irora, they themselves.
yx, &c., used separately, are used definitely, with emphasis.
irasie, for what reason?
kī, I'm in doubt about.
iyi, or *irora*, he is the one that is accountable, or they are accountable.

VERB.

The substantive is wanting.
yx igko, I (am) here.
Nouns are converted into verbs by prefixing the syllables *um*, *men* in the ind. mood, pres. tense, thus—
nimpai, fence.
ya umnimpai, I am fencing.
kik em nimpai,

iyi umnimpai,
nelĕntugi, love.
ya umnelintugi, I love.
kik em nelintugi,
iyi um nelintugi.
talugi, netemi talugi, a murderer.
ya (k) umintalugi, I kill.
kik emĭn talugi. Nouns commencing with *n* take *um*, and with *t*, *mĭn*, as *tai*, *mintai*, *taru*, *mintaru*. Several take *mán*, *mand*, *mem*, &c.
The rule is not of much use, as it does not hold in the formation of other tenses and moods where it undergoes many changes.

ADVERBS.

Of Time —
   irē, to-day.   *irē*, to-day.
   mran, to-morrow.   *minu*, yesterday, &c.
   weme, day after to- *no'eme*.
     morrow.   *no'inag*.
   winag, 4 days hence. *no'impi*.
   wimpe, 5 days hence. *no'isas*.
   wisas, 6 days hence.
   nemindog, rest.
   marima, now.
   etuai, some time ago.

itetuai, itnimperis, of old.
pol sugku, when.
lap, while ; *our lap,* by and by.
pole ku, a while.
indowi, continuously.
dō indowi, without resting or stopping.
Imp.—*ŭnum,* quick.
penuri, afterward, after.
nimpugon, time.
nimpugon deve, how many times ?
sai nimpugon, one time.
nimpugon sai (indef.,) future.
mante lap, after awhile, from *mante,* to abide.
it-e-marima, now for the first, not formerly.
uvum, without end.
uvum nevi su, years without end.
poarap, evening ; *poakas,* forenoon.
poakas-poakas, noon.
prubokom, morning.
pumrok atunenemes, midnight.

Of Place—
igko, here ; *nimpe,* there (near.)
yui, there (remote) ; *ilampe,* yonder.
isut, far away ; *aitugo,* remote.
isut wokon, very far off.
ratekompe, over there.

ratekomisa, up there.
ratekomiep, down there.
potifot, near, short.
nugkon umpe, beyond.
nugkon un pelum, on this side.
nugkon nu, across or over the water.
tan, the back ; *tan nugkon,* other side of the island.

Of Asking—
  ia, where ? *yēi,* where (is he) ?
  nigai, when ? (past and future.)
  deve, how many ?
  dērego, how many of each ?
  nokowo, how ? *itokowo,* which ?
  irantie, irasie, why ? why should ?
  wantie, wasie, what may, &c.
  kamsugi, kampose ugi, to what purpose ?
  kumnēa, where (you) from ?
  nimsin tie, for what purpose ?
  wamē, who of us ? &c.
  wamē-e-mē, pl.
  wantie, what about, for ?
  ōwo, what is the matter ?
  ōwo mas, what was the cause of his death ?
  ku or ? (or is it otherwise.) Used when a question is asked indirectly.

Of Affirmation, &c.—
monokowo, yes.
ēyi, no (nothing,) never mind.
tawi, no, not (emphatic.)
oo, indicates assent.
osog nam, truly, he has made good his word.
itnesog, true, truth.
sugku, thus, as.
unipmi, before, in the presence of.
unĭmtum, before thee, in thy sight.
eve, go thou.
etu ve, go (thou) not.

PREPOSITIONS.
ra, in, on, to, &c., for, from.
gi, ugi, about, concerning, with, by means of.
u, un, urun, in towards, under, in company with (sing.)
dal, with (plural.)
nimsin, for.
umsog, within.
ratunisog, within, inside of.
ilat, out.
ratelat, outside.
nisikon (declinable,) for the use, benefit of one.

en, of, belonging to.
ilebo teven, in the midst, go, over.
ra mumpon, under, in (as in a ship,) on a table.
ra netugon, under (as under a table.)
ran tan, on the back.
impuap, underneath.
imiluo, on high.
it, for (origin primary reason.)
it nigai, when (was its beginning.)
it sah, upward.
it sep, downward.
it lum, towards.
it lap, delay.
it lah, fromwards.
it wi, little.
menakanwi, to hate a little.
potipot go, each (every one) is short.
po, pun, pug, signs of dative.
ra, ran, ira, signify the object unto or against which a thing is done.

CONJUNCTIONS.

m, connective (inseparable,) contraction of *im*, and; *ku*, or; *nagku*, if; *popōwo*, because ; *kō*. but, notwithstanding ; *mō*, the *o* indicates sequence, consecution (afterward or again.)

INTERJECTIONS.

ah, O !
pah, (disagreeable.)
ipe, (pleasure.)
ōva, (indeed, is it so ?)
upo, (wonder.)
uwo, when your remark was not apprehended or misunderstood.
uwē, (pain.)
u, rising inflection, answer when a person is called by name, thus, *Nalig? u!*

IDIOMS.

devego, how many of each ?
sai tevego, one only of each.
umagkip unipmi, to be impudent (lit. to fly in the face.)
e ko sai, alone.
kimnēa, where art thou, or are you from ?
kĭm ampēa, where are you going ?

EROMANGAN DIALECTS.

I. Yoku or Enyx (pop. 1000?) II. Sie or Sorng (2000?) III. (500?) IV. Utaha (nearly extinct, 50?) V. Novūl-Amleg (extinct.)

(.g denotes hard g.)

	III. Ura.	IV. Utaha.
1	sī	sokc
2	ˌgelu	kalū
3	ˌgeheli	kĭhĭli
4	lemelu	lemelu
5	sūorem	sūkrim
6	misī	sĭmsokc
7	sĭmhelu	simnalu
8	sĭmheli	sĭmniheli
9	sĭnivat	simnivat
10	lūrem	narōlem
11	lurem mitaperigi pa sai	narolem otam nugo sokc
12	lurem mitaperigi pa gelu	
20	lurem gelū	narolem kalū
100	lurem lūrem	

EROMANGAN LANGUAGE.

URA.

I, &c.	My, &c.	To, or against me, &c.
yx	ari yx	bo yx
ˌga	ari ka	bu ka
iyi	ariyi	buh ni
gim	ari ˌgim	bukim
gis (In.)	ari ˌgis (In.)	bukis
gimi	ari ˌgemi	buh nimi
lēl	ahlēl	buh nil

UTAHA.

I, &c.	My, &c.	To me, &c.	For me = my benefit.
yō	etiyo	pi yō	neseko
kō	eteko	pig ko	nesekum
iyi	et iyi	pini	
kum	etekum	pig kum	
ˌgis (In.)	etiˌgis	pig kis	
kimi	etekimi	pig kimi	
yoril	eteyoril	pig kor	nesekira
			nesekar, feast

yamu, this
yumu, that
yumu yu, these

yō im pe yō, I myself
kom peg ko, thou thyself
iyi pe iyi   [&c.

80 GRAMMAR OF THE

wi, who?
uwi, (pl.)?
etuwi, whose?

yoril im pe yoril
yuki, here
tavewe, not = *tawa*

nimpeyigo, now

aha, where?
nugo, when?

kimnaha, where have you come from?

The changes from Yoku to Sie are slight. Y. tiē, S. siē; sukrim, siklim; virok, vilik; nahiven, nasiven; hū, sī; nitnin, etni. II. Sorug. Sorug, my; sorum, thy; isen, his; sorit our, (In.;) soremam, our; soremi, your; isenda, their; *sie*, what? *irasie*, for what? *siema*, that which; *ōvun siē*, things, effects, property.

URA.—VERB.

Nogori, to know.

yx no͵gori	yx o͵gori, I knew, recently
͵ga kene͵gori	͵ga o͵gori
iyi ko͵gori	iyi o͵gori
͵gimuh no͵gori	yx no͵gori, I knew, past
͵guh no͵gori (In.)	yx no͵gori, I will know
gimi kĭh no͵gori	
lēl kih no͵gori	
	ya amenda, I abide
guh urim no͵gori (In.)	ga kamenda

EROMANGAN LANGUAGE.

gim urim no͟gori
kĭh no͟gori
lēl ĭh no͟gori

yx um amli, I speak

iyi ͟gamenda
͟gŭ lemenda
͟gisu lemenda
gimi ki lemenda
lēl ͟gi lemenda
͟gim URA menda
͟gis ura' menda
͟gimi kiremenda
lēl giremenda

UTAHA.—VERB.

1. yo ĭm no͟gori
2. ko kum nohgori
3. iyi umnokgori
1. ku lem nogori
1. gis lem nogori
2. kimi kimel nogori
3. yoril elem nogori
   kutem nohgori
   gis etem nohgori
2. kik elem = kimi kik elem, &c.
3. yoril elem

1. ya okori, &c.

URA.

nihmi umugkum, sun
umōva, moon
umse, stars

UTAHA.

nimnim ugkum, sun
umse, stars
novonx, sea

URA.

nīyī, sky
wavelx, wind
nebip, rain
de, sea
yarumne, chief
yirema, man
ariareven, woman
nalalx, boy
uhnomu, fish
nelī, ship
nc, water
lxepe, tall
urekīs, sharp
lamapa, large
nahlēīmpa, sleep
ureverek, war
dīyīye, peace
Uvo, God
dugkorowo, laugh
nari, feast
wat, sin
novulu, word
avowat-ur, bad
nehni, son

UTAHA.

yatumu, chief
umu, fish
uyu, water
nahlumrag, sleep
utuvorekil, war
Uyo, God
rat, sin
novil, word
avensokc (lavugsokc, pl.,) my brother
nōkuwī, tree
timen (timo = nate) father
tupmis, plantation
yamu, this
yumu, that
yumuyu, these
yo ĭm pe yō, I, myself
kom peg ko, thou, thyself, &c.
iyi pe iyi
yoril ĭm pe yoril
wi, who? (uwi, pl.)
etuwi, whose?
aha, where?

EROMANGAN LANGUAGE.

URA.
vin, sister
afrō, my friend
avoksī, my brother
nyi, tree
sī gan, one only
rimen (dera = nate) father
livan, wife
xin, husband
umitar, rainbow
dughmus, plantation
dena, ground

UTAHA.
nugo, when?
kimnaha, where have you come from?
novx, cocoanut
unde, blood
iso, spear,
levenahan, bow
nelin, dan
atnelō = lo eni, his canoe
atnelŏ, his people
yuki, here
tavewe, not = tawi
yore, to-day
etninu, yesterday
etnuwoseme, &c.
etnuwosimpe
polebu, to-morrow
xwo, &c.

THE LORD'S PRAYER.

I. YOKU.—Itemen-e-kam unpokup, ete tumpora nin-e-kik, elum lō enugkik : eti numpi natekisah en taru enugkik ra nemap sugku pe unpokup : ovug kam irē pen dan nevag aremī nisekomam : mefielĭntug kam sat su enugkam, sugku ka kĭm lafielĭu tok-onda sat su isenda mori su umnumpi sat iramam; etu tōro-kam ran tapmi, ko simsimpari iramam marugi sat. It enugkik lō ĭm horog ĭm nilasilaswi enugkik, uvum nevi su, ĭndōwi, ĭndōwi. Amen.

II. Sorug.—Eti tumpora nin sorum—taru sorum—sat su soremam—It sorem lō.

III. Ura.—Rimen ˌgim unīyī : erigi uvuhnumu nivana ˌga : enim nel araka : erigi numbu nerigiyek araka ran dena suku ara nīyī : ovo kim yeramba nelin neven aremī san ˌgim : efielenigi ˌgim nareki wat su arakim suku ˌgureneligi lēl nareki wat su ahlēl mori gira numbu wat arani gim : etu tambuni ˌgim ran dahmi, kō ambarē arigkim marugi nareki wat: popowosa nelō arika, im atam, im nilaswi, arika numgī niliya, uvo, uvo. Amen.

IV. Utaha.—Timen-e-kum unpokup : etura sum nin eteko : enim namu nelō : ete numpu natekimoresah mintaru ra yumup sugku pe unpokup : ovig kum yore pe nelin nevug aramī nisekum : efielinigkum eturat yu etekum sugku kutem afielinig kor eturat yu eteyoril mori elumpu eturat iramim : metu toreg kum ra tapmi, ko simsimpari iramim malini eturat : popōwose namu nelō, ĭm horog, ĭm nilasuwi eteko, uvum nevi yu, ĭndōwi, ĭndōwi. Amen.

SKETCH

OF THE

SANTO GRAMMAR AND VOCABULARY.

ARTICLE.

Ne, ĭ. te, i, separable, as *ne leman,* a man ; *ne gēi,* a woman ; *te tulu,* the three ; *ĭ nigo,* thou. *Ne* is also used definitely as *ne lepa,* the earth ; *ne tuua,* a person (indefinite ;) *mo i Iofa* and Jehovah ; *i* is another form of *ĭ. Ie* and *ai* are definite.

NOUN.

GENDER.—*Leman,* man ; *gēai,* woman (Valpay dialect *ne kepai* ;) *ne dura leman,* a man child ; *ne dura gēai,* a woman child. *Tata,* father ; *meme,* mother, applied by children to their own parents. *Timana,* his father ; *tinana,* his mother ; *imana,* her brother (applied by a sister ;) *imx,* my brother ; *manena,* his brother.

NUMBER is indicated by the particle *ro,* as, *ro leman,* men ; *ro gēai,* women ; *ro tuua,* people ;

F

ro dura, children ; *ro leman lima*, five men ; *ro tuu ta*, bushmen ; *ro wogi*, no more ; *urenezunoki*, all ; *ta wērē*, plenty ; *tarias tarius*, multitudes : *vas vas* indicates many, as, *vas tuua*, many people : *purun moa*, a great many ; *purun moa lo lo lo*, very many ; *tarias ruan pa*, innumerable.

 Case.—*Patuu*, my head
   putum, thy head
   putuna, his head
   putu rua, our two heads (inclusive)
   putumurua, our two heads (exclusive)
   putumrua, your two heads
   putururua, their two heads
   puturie, our heads (inclusive)
   putumamam, our heads
   putumiu, your heads
   puturire, their heads

This is the nominal suffix ; the next shows the separate or emphatic possessive :—

   poi nou, my pig
   poi nom, thy pig
   poi noana, his pig

poi no rua, poi nomurua, poi nomrua, poi no rie (inclusive.)

poi no mam, our pig
poi no miu, your pig
poi no rire, their pig

Tux, my friend ; *tuom, tuana, tuurua, tuom—urua, tuomrua, tu rurua, tuutulu, tuumutulu, tuumtulu, turitulu,*

a tuorie (inclusive)
a tuamam, our friend
a tuamiu, your friend
a tuarire, their friend

Ro tuu *ki* Wulua, "men of Wulua;" *Venux,* my house ; *ovou,* my ship ; *tata nou,* my father.

The word in the objective follows the verb that governs it unchanged, as *na veti nigina,* I speak to him ; *nigin keli lep,* he digs the ground ; *na lolou uli suri nigo,* I my heart (inside) pained on account of thee ; *na lolou leli suri nigo,* I love thee ; I – my inside—(is) comely on account of thee ; *ko sami me o,* come (up) with me ; *ore nigina,* call him ; *no doroni lep ko i sule, mo sap simai me ne serina,* I draw a line up to (as far as) the stone, and not to the foot of him.

ADJECTIVES.

Mertai, good; *ta leli*, comely, agreeable; *oovun*, bad, worthless; *mertai val val saki* better? *mertai lulusu*, best; *vile mertai val val siwo*, less good; *leman mertai*, a good man; *ruana kx ta leli*, a pretty flower.

Numerals—		(Walua d.	
1	tewa	ketea	
2	rua	kerua	
3	tulu	kitulu	
4	vate	kwati	
5	lima	kilima	
6	ono	kaioni	
7	pitu	kaipitu	
8	olu	kaialu	
9	diwo	kaisua	
10	sunuvulu	sunuvulu)	
11	sunuvulu rav tewa		
20	novulu rua		
21	novulu rav tewa		
30	novulu tulu		
31	novulu tu rav tewa		
40	novulu vati		
41	novulu vati rav tewa		
100	lēl vaka tewa		

101 lēl vakatewa raven tewa
200 lēl vakarua
201 lēl vakarua mo raven tewa
1,000 ruwun tewa
10,000 ruwun sunuvulu
100,000 tarias ruwun pa, innumerable thousands, or thousands manifold

ORDINALS.—

vakatewana, first
vakaruana, second
vakatulina, third
vakavatina, fourth
vakalimana, fifth, &c.

TIMES —

vakatewa, once
vakarua, twice
vakatulu, three times
vakavati, four times
vakalima, five times, &c.

Wuti tewa, daily once ; *wuti rua*, every second day ; *wuti tulu*, every third day ; *pon in wuti tewa*, once a day ; *pon in wuti rua*, every second day.

SANTO GRAMMAR

PRONOUNS.

PERSONAL.—

Singular —

nx, na, I
nigo, thou
nigina, he

Dual—

urua, we two (inclusive)
umurua, we two
umrua, you two
ru rua, they two

Trial—

utulu, we three (Inclusive)
umutulu, we three
umtulu, you three
ri tulu, they three

Plural—

rie we, (inclusive)
emam, we
emiu, you
rirē, they

Possessive —
nou, my
nom, thy
noana, his
no urua, ours, two (Inclusive)
nomurua, ours two
nomrua, yours two
no rurua, theirs two
no rie, ours (Inclusive)
nomam, ours
nomiu, yours
norire, theirs

RELATIVE.—None; the personal used instead.

INTERROGATIVE.—*i se*, who? *ro se*, who (plural)? *ne sai*, what? *no i se*, whose? *gin ot, e kin ot*, this or this? which? *momo*, how?

DEMONSTRATIVE.—*kin oti*, this; *rir'oti*, these; *rir'oti ini*, these here; *rir'oti evanu*, those over there.

INDEFINITE—*Ris mei*, some; *sap rots*, not many; *sapetesi*, no, not, none; *zi*, or *zizi tewa*, just one; *te tewa*, the, just one; *vasgena*, by himself; *vasgiu*, by myself, *vasgim*, by thyself; *vasgi rie* (Inclusive,) we, by ourselves; *vasgemam*, *vasgemiu*, *vasgirire:* this may be *vas ke nox, vas ke rire; vas* indicates plurality—many—an indefinite number; *ki,* belonging to. If such is the analysis it means the plural is confined to *me,* or to *them,* a definite number of persons; *k* and *g* are used indiscriminately.

VERB.

The substantive appears to be *kin* or *gin,* to which is joined the adverb of place, *ini;* thus, *ni vie,* or *viai,* where art thou; *no kinini,* I am here; or, *no ini,* I (am) here; *nigin ine,* he (is) there.

The indicative mood is presented thus— Present tense, *venai,* to come (on a level;) *samai,* to come up; *simai,* to come down *(timai;)* present tense with *mini,* now; singular, *no vena mini,* I come, am coming
        ni vena mini, thou comest, art coming
        nigin vena mini, he comes, is coming

Dual—
    urua vena mini (Inclusive)
1 *umurua vena mini*
2 *umrua vena mini*
3 *rurua vena mini*

Trial—
> *utulu vena mini* (Inclusive)
> 1 *umutulu vena mini*
> 2 *umtulu vena mini*
> 3 *ri tulu vena mini*

Plural—
> *rie vena mini* (Inclusive)
> 1 *emam vena mini*
> 2 *emiu vena mini*
> 3 *rire vena mini*

No venai, I came, past tense; *nx to venai,* I will come, future; *no to vano,* I will go; *te amo nx to mule,* afterwards I will go; *no mule mini,* I go now; *lako,* to go; *no lako,* I went; *nigo lako,* you went; *nx to lako,* I will go; *no lako mini,* I go, or am going now; *nigin sap simai,* he came not; *nigin lako te posai, nigin lako maa posai,* he went to (or, for to) deceive; *ko mule,* go (singular;) *emi mule,* go ye. Particles used with verbs, *te, ti, to, ma, mo, maa, amo, towai; rire lakai,* they went up (as a river.)

ADVERBS.

Of Time.—
> *nogovune,* to-day
> *pwanovi,* to-morrow

pon rua, two days hence
pon tulu, &c.
nonori, yesterday
pon go ro rua, day before yesterday
pon go ro tulu, &c.

Pogo runi, sunset; *mine*, now; *ta mine*, long ago (?); *pogorune*, near sunset; *perperi toko*, recently, a day or two (ago); *na rakatewa*, presently; *alpaku*, by and by; *tea, team*, subsequently; *pwa*, after a while, soon; *tx*, soon, in a little; *ta minmintuge*, and *tamim*, future; *tor rakatewa*, just now; *tup tewa*, continuously; *ron tup tewa*, always day; *lirgan i elo*, midday; *puni*, dusk; *metanal rer saki*, after sunrise; *metanal punu*, sunset; *al metua*, 9 a.m.; *rorgoro*, morning, dawn; *rorrori*, twilight, *raka wuti tewa*, sometimes; *rakavakatewa*, presently; *tuai ron tuge kopkopu*, sunrise.

Of Place.—*ini*, here; *inē*, there; *kenia* (in reply;) *eranu*, over there (near;) *evantuge*, far away; *tetaruara*, at hand, near; *ral* denotes position; *val siwo*, below; *val re siwo*, underneath; *te saki*, the top, upper part; *val re saki*, above, upper side; *me ne uluna*, on the outside; *me ne lolona*, in the inside; *me ne gapa*, within, between; *me ne togema*, on the back, *me ne gisina*, before, in the presence of; *me ne porerana*, at the side.

Of Inquiry.—*vie, viai,* where? *nenesa,* when? (past;) *pwanesa,* when? (future;) *ne sai,* what? *te visa,* how many? *mo.* what did you say? *temwam,* why? *suri temo,* on what account? *aworsai,* why? (reprovingly;) *e?* (in asking indirectly;) *suri sai,* what reason? *e! se enia,* who is there? *sogona sai,* what like? how?

Tasi expresses repetition.

Of Affirmation.—*e,* yes; *oa, e! ou,* no; *sapetesi,* no, by no means; also *sap* [Efate *tiba,* dialect *tab*;] *a,* rising inflection, answer to a call; *i,* falling inflection, I don't know; *ĭ,* rising inflection, denial, inarticulate; *sogona,* so, like; *sogon gini,* it was just so; *kinai,* quite so; *ko,* sign of imperative; *ko,* as far as; *tev toko,* equal; *io,* yes (Wulua.)

PREPOSITIONS.

Me, in, by; *de,* in, along, on; *me,* with; *ki,* belonging to; *suri,* on account of, about, &c.; *livgana,* between; *me ne livgana,* in the midst; *me ne ruruan,* on the surface.

CONJUNCTIONS.

Mo, and ; *'e*, or ; *urunan*, because ; *ni teer riai*, you come from where ? *ni de ra toko*, you go where ?

Vas kiu, I alone.
ras kim, thou alone.
ras gena, he alone,
&c.

English.	Santo.*	Efate.
abba	tata	mama, abu
abide	toloko	toko, to, matoko, fatoko
able	suinai	
accept	lēa lô	uisi, tabe
adultery	kurkuri ; van mēa	tauso
afflict	kôd matea	meri sa ki, bati sa ki
afraid	wotoa, wotwotoa	mataku
air	ivivi	nin
alive	mēuri, memeur toko	mauri, mole
all (none left)	rowogi, wunwun ôgi lô vunia	bakauti, mau
almighty	vasvas suinai	

* Note.—Mr. Gordon's *ŋ* = *p*w, and *d* = *ts*.

English.	Santo.	Efate.
also	sogona	mero (again)
altar	sauive	
always	tup tewa	ti makot (not cease)
alone	vas kiu ; vasgena (vas ki na ?)	sikigu, sikina
above	saki ; siwo, below	elag ; *saki*, to go up ; *siuo*, to go down
arrive	tivu	bakilina (come in sight)
anger	lolon kegara lolon ein were lolon melum	maieto, namaietoa
anoint	môgi niu	burei, alofi
answer	tami	bisa (speak)
any	te zi tev	te, tete
another	zi tuai	te pota, karua
apart	vesves ari	misal
appear	rer saki	bakilina
arise	tup saki	tulena
arouse	mematai *	bugoni (wake up)
arrow	newusu (Wu. vina)	ne tipa, nausu (reed)
ascend	saki	saki

* Wu., *i.e.* Wulua dialect of Santo ; Va., Valpay dialect ; Er. stands for Eromangan.

English.	Santo.	Efate.
ashamed	mulin toko	maliere
ask	tin lepwī	tatago, bitali
	vet lepwī	
	tenc sopsop genia	
asleep	jinaru ; jiranu	maturu
assemble	seri	saisai
astonished	ôsnôki	maga (gape)
anchor	dur tesiwo	namtau
	riptuogi-taraoni	
hearken	emi roron toko	rogo
attend	sēri ; sap sēri	taki torogo

Animals —

rat	keriu	kusue
lizard	malwud	äo
whale	suum-lôsi	tafura
shark	kumiru	bako
pig	poi	d. wak, wago
flies	puloa	lago
strange bird	toa ato	
bad	ne tuua vet worô-gi (Va. kokovun) imo, a! imi api vovun; ta vovun; mania lolon sap (pl. lēli)	sa

AND VOCABULARY. 99

ENGLISH.	SANTO.	EFATE.
bamboo	lumuô	lobu
barren	wuiaru	ruma
battle	lus api	na fakal
	Er. novohat	
bear	vol saki	sela
bear	wērwera ; papi ; pēpai	
beat	lusi	boka
beauty	ta lēli	
beautiful	lon sara puse pus	meta uia, uia
begin	moig	
beginning	ne moig ?	
believe	taluia, aataluto kai	seralesoko
bent (crooked)	qakqakēli	tageli, takelkel
beseech	tĭntĭn lapi	fira, serei
beg	tĭntĭn lapi	tago, bitaga
betray	pospos api	belak tautau
bewail	tôn pulpa	tagisi
bind	kedai	seli
bird	toa	manu, *toa* fowl
bite	kotkot	kati, katikati
billows	tos lelav ; tôse	re ron na beau

English.	Santo.	Efate.
bless	umi.; ooi	bisa uia (speak good)
blew	susuvui	
big	tugalav	lebaleba, bipila
blind	mat oora, mat meri	barea, meta barea
blood	megavina	rā, trā
blossom	virana kx	na buma na kasu
blot out	dôrdôrvaia	nunu
blow out	sunwi matēa	sui bunu
blows	susuvui, conch; lôn sēriv, wind	sui baigo, conch; lagi sau. wind
boar	rawē	uago anoi, tapare
body	epena	na batoko (na)

Members of

(*a*) External—

Eromanga.	Santo.	Efate.
body—		
nokolisiran	epena	na batoko na
skin—		
nokolistan	kurina	na uili na, d. *kuli*
head—		
numpug-n	potuna	na bau na

Eromanga.	Santo.	Efate.
hair—		
novlimpu	wuluna	na lulu na
crown—		
numpulepes	pilona	na masua na
forehead—		
nafinîn	panona	na rai na
ear—		
telugon	anlana	na taliga na
eye, face—		
nipmi-nimtug	metana (Wu. marontra)	na meta na
apple—		
yaloorok	livgan metan lon metan	bul meta na
eyebrow—		
utagin vet	puspusan metan	na fasu na meta na
eyelash—		
novlipmi	sosop pun metan	
cheek—		
wx nugun	palena	na babu na
chin—		
nasiwan	asena	na asi na

G

Eromanga.	Santo.	Efate.
beard—		
novolugon	kumim	na lulu na asina
lips—		
nokolugon	vivina (lower) val vi (upper)	na goli na
nose—		
worokolag	nonona (Wu. mansuntra)	na gusu na
mouth—		
naveram	wowana	na uaka na
neck—		
nowan	alona	na noa na
shoulder—		
nivlokon	ririna	na bamu na
arm—		
nilepen nokoben	ne rana	na aru na
elbow—		
yx uga	suguna	na uisi ki aru na
wrist—		
itemelokwi	malo gina liman	
thumb—		
uvunomu	tatopwin	kin leba

AND VOCABULARY. 103

EROMANGA.	SANTO.	EFATE
finger—		
dugerugon	rara ona liman	na kini na
palm—		
	lolona limana	na mele eru na
nail—		
fetnatpu	pisuna	tapales na kini na
hand—		
nokoben	limana (Wu. lemantra) vaka metuo (right) vaka merx (left)	na aru na, d. lima na matua maure
bosom—		
nemindugon	soltana	na ruma na
breasts—		
ni	lulu, lolon	susu na
back—		
tan	pulina	na taku na
back-bone—		
nesisi	kon pulina	na matu na
belly—		
netnin	tiana	na peli na

EROMANGA.	SANTO.	EFATE.
navel—		
yumput		na buto na
thigh—		
nevan	wodana, denina	na mäo na
leg—		
nelepon nō won	tian palona	na tuo na
knee—		
numpumteren	wun poun	na batua na
foot—		
nōwon	serina	na tuo na
sole		
mumpon no-won	lolon serina	na mele na tuo na
instep		
tan nowon	pulin serina	na taku natuo na
flesh		
fan	visgona	na bakasi na
tongue—		
niluamen	memena	na mena na

(*b*) Internal, &c.

AND VOCABULARY.

EROMANGA.	SANTO.	EFATE.
bone— novian	suina	na fatu na
rib— nimperi	porerana	fiti
bowels— nalniniwara	tinena	marite
heart— umpatemōnōk	wowa kad kad gina	am kanoa ; po
lungs— mampatevanu		amo
liver— nugkilemil	mapwena	tale kabu
teeth— nugon-neleven	petina	bati
veins— narep		
blood— de	megavina	ra
tears— nulipmi	tensina	riri meta
sweat— nenora		toru

106 SANTO GRAMMAR

EROMANGA.	SANTO.	EFATE.
windpipe— worumnōk	pulan lumuo	
fat— nup (flesh)	ruina	bakas tare
lard— nigaku		
gall—	midina	na konei na
gall bladder—	tolgo suna	uli kokon
throat—	rigingana	
hip—	polena	
bread-fruit	(Wu-lewu)	bitau, bitam, bitaf
bird	toa	manu
beak	petina	goli
spur	luuna	
comb	pulan keka	teretere
gizzard	vetuna	
feathers	kavil(g) kĭna, quill	afaru, mau
wings	kavena	afaru
book	kanutu; lanlanutu	tusi (Samoan)
boil	sēsara	tunu
born	papi; pepi	

English.	Santo.	Efate.
bottom	qapa; lolona	pago
bow	vini (Wu. tôo) (Er. nefani)	āsu
bread	kuv gugu (Er. yōup)	kabu, koau
break	ul motia (as thread;) utia	gote, kote
breath	ususuna manmanostoko	maro
bright	tugi le ululia rinrinoka	girigiri
bring	ko lo venai	buat ia mai
bridge	ne vali	
brink	qanqan ona woro siv tuge	tiki
brook	nopu	noai sera
burn	suli	tubara ki; sulu
bush	lolon gx	na kasu, d. kau
buy	wuli; wulwula	bakot
bushmen	ro tu uta	nakan uta
brushwood	qerqeri	
bracelet	pandum	baniban (armlet)
bottle	ne puruua	
begin	ko tutun tupwai ko tutun lili gini	

English.	Santo.	Efate.
clouds	(Wu. oo ; Va. neko)	tai na lagi
cocoanut	(Wu. kolo : Va. metui)	aniu
call	ore	so
chase	peli	koba
calm	rorontoko	tamate
cave	qupa malo poqan malo (Er. neveli)	falea
gullies	poqan to lako	paloa
carry	sol	sela, d. sola
catch	kidia	buati
cautiously	melum—geniu	malua, d. mailum
chain	os kia	mae ni fatu
chastise	ao soso oronia ?	sumati
chirp	kotkotu	
cheat	va kar posina	suru (deceive)
chief	mul, mulisa	uota
white	wuo-tugilgila	tare
cloth	ovpai	kalu
clothe	rure	su gori
coals	ro pudale ove	
club	wada	pwe, d. mbat
cold	wurwuraka	milate

English.	Santo.	Efate.
cool	memawo	milate
come	sami, simai, vanai (Er. umampelum)	mai, bano mai
come again	venvenari	mero mai
colours	wuo-lov	
white	lovu	tare
black	metu	gota, d. maeta
red	kgara (?)	miel
blue	malgedgej	milakesa
yellow	tamena	monamona
green	mul ve sakai mai	milakesa, kesakesa
comfort	umia ; aa memwesia	bakali
command	megui	tupa
company	la ururtoko	saisai
conclusion	resi	nu
confusion	wowosi	bunufunoi
continue	totoko (Er. umante)	toko
cooking	vevalx ; au kana	tai
countenance	qanon api	meta, rai
covet	taru irirea	miseroa, meta makura
count	tutuni	fe

English.	Santo.	Efate.
counter-mand	zi a vanu	tupa goro
cross	kad ve e logi	kasu beltagot
crumbs	ean kan meliga numiti	na feroa
crucify	tura vilvilia te van me ne ko ta kad ve e logi	turia nakasu beltagot
crowd	tokowonwono	taua
cry	toni	kei, tagi
cure	mog ginia, mog gini am to leli	bakamauri
curse	(vet) nagavira	bisa sa ki
custom	zi mat wunena	supe
cut	dimi ; tavia	tefe
curly hair	wul melum, wul memelu	
club	wad gin lulus api, wad gin supwe	
damsel	susara keai	tara
dance	sawe	sali
dazzle	kopkopo	
day	roni—pon	aliati
last day	ron tuptogi	aliati etaku mau
dead	mati	mate

English.	Santo.	Efate.
deaf	anlan putu mogmoga	taliga paro
dear	lolon lelai	metana i lebaleba
deceit	posposé	bisuru, suru, seli
deny	koronogi kigia	goro, koro
desire	taru matea, tara irirea, covet	mesau
dig	keli lep	kili
disciples	ro tuua lulu rire vanai	
dish	wea	siloa
dip	wea	bugi
distant	esatuge, evantuge	emai, toga
disobey	til wol lol oora pearaka til wol tamtam pupura peri rak	rog biri, rog tao
disperse	medala	tabera ki
distribute (as food)	konwunwuni	bakarau
do	aoa ; aa sogon to lea—don't take	bati, meri, brigi
dog	wurin	kuri
draw	levaia	lafi, urusa

English.	Santo.	Efate.
dream	metur-popori	libi na pore
drink	oomia (Va. un)	minu, munu
drive	iso	tia
drought	alwora	us tika, elo leba-leba
drown	meiriri	minu in tas
drunk	metan moololi	mate ki na maluk (kafa)
water	ra?	noai, nai, nivai, d. ran
elephantiasis	pura	i buria, mutra
eat	genia; gongoni (Va. koka)	kani, kanikani, bami
embrace	gadgadai	
end	wul la mine	na meta pago
the earth	ne lepa (Wu. ono; Va. tano)	tano; *leba* clay
enemy	ne val vekalo	ualu pota
equal	tev toko	to sikei
unequal	veduna	bisār
exchange	dondona	auli
fall	vidonia; wora	roa (rowa,) tarupaki

AND VOCABULARY. 113

ENGLISH.	SANTO.	EFATE.
fear	wotoa, wotwotia, wotunia	mataku
feast	supwe	in tamate, d. pelaki
	(Er. nesekar, narïgari)	
fence	pala	koro
fan	iria	nifi
feign	sumopai	bisuru
fever	veveo	na misaki
fight	var vini sesori api	fiatu, batinafakal
	(Er. umnavohat)	
firmament	wase gin tolon	elagi
	(Er. uneai, pokup)	
fish	ravrav iga (Wu. mad = fish)	na ika
fish-scales	ne	nun naika
fisherman	tuua gin iga	
flame	serai toko	mena na kabu
flies	lano	lango
flow	owu	sera
float	sale ser toko mene rurun pe	sali
full	pe tata were vas tata weri	bura
follow	pal suri	rausi, usi

English.	Santo.	Efate.
forbid	korgoroa	koro
forget	sap lim toni; lolon oora	rara tan ia
forgive	oomkorgorogi	
forsake	umdurogogi	turu bis ia
fruit	pegini touna, tou nekou	ua, d. weti
garden	verx; kokoo	atalemate
gate	wawo	likau
generation	(tok) ol	tago
gift	wudon worogi; lo worogi	nafituan
girdle	matun	tali
give	lelapi; kik towi wudon worogi	tu
glad	degia	maro, laelae
glass	titiro (looking)	titiro
go	va; lako; mule ba, ban (Wu. noa)	
good	lol ta lele; mertai uia	
great	pul pa (Er. nusian, horog, tamas)	lebaleba, bipila
grief	lolon uli lolon te kidia	rogtesa

English.	Santo.	Efate.
grief	lolon te egi	
	lolon supwolia	
grate	rasa	
grindstone	sul rasrasa	nafa
grew to manhood	meur saki leman	
gratitude	merti ; lolon leli	
gulf	qap dondona	
hard	melgx moa	kasua
haste	la wuswusog toko	marafi
hat	sunim	tapau
health	lel toko	uia toko, rogteauia
hear	ronoa ; ron didi liona	rogo
hearken	ron toko ; ronron pupuri	rogo, taki rogosa ki
heat	tutun	bitunu
help	wodoi, todori ko wodio, help me	auli (take place of)
house,	venua (Wu. ima)	suma
hide	susurpunu vi punpunu	pelu, tasuruki

English.	Santo.	Efate.
honest	vul gin te tiv toko (a fair bargain) vet vi goil sake (an overcharge)	uia, folofolo lena
hunger	tiana se raprapa	bitelo
husk	kurina	uili na
insecure	mosmosug	
innumer- able	tarias ro an pa	man taparoparo
innocent	pil vet woronia	tika nauisien sa
image	qanx, qanom	
imitate	asusuia	bakauli
idle, lazy	suin melum	malo
infant	potiena	totau
insects	kerkerako	
inn	komali venua me neko- mali	
joy	lolonasaki lulu rirai sake	semasema, laelae, maro
jealousy	nakapura nakapurio, of me	atakasua
jump	sesale	soka
knife	dimi	misimis, mās

AND VOCABULARY. 117

English.	Santo.	Efate.
kill	lusi	bati bunu, atu
kiss	dumia	sumi
kick	piligia	pia
know	pisia	atae
	ronoa pis tokai	
	mat pisi	
	lolon ron tokai	
not know	saparoa lolona	ti atae
kind	omi ; aa mosi	sau uia, popo uia
kava	wosi	maluk
leave off	ko lo tuogi	turu bisi
let go	durtuogi	tao, turu bisi
let it stop	sogon toko	i ga tok
lightning	ledmari	fili
live	memeuri	mauri, mole
light	alo	aliati, na mirama
	zinzina (moon)	
	memeram	
	pula, pulom	
lead	levlev	meraki
lance	tavia	ola
lose	vidoni matea	bati buele
long time hence	tuai ron tuge	tuai

H

English.	Santo.	Efate.
lights	pula	sulu
laugh	mana	muru
look up	tetaa sake	lo saki, le saki
look down	cer siwo	lo siuo, le sua
look round	ilo vanu	lo tal, le tal
lie by the fire	nonowusme neovi	tilei na kabu
lean	wearaka	tabe
limp	tigo	
lads	perai ulwo	karikiki
moon	wula; wul wotu (new)	atelag
more	mono	
no more	sabeti tuai mono	te leba (enough)
meet	qanovia; rarponwi	sua, tilasi
mimic	sorsor towai	bakauli
mark	doronia	mitiri
music	pepulala ne viga	
man	leman	nata, natamole (living man)
maimed	pupu	
mat	epa	namit
make	tarea (Wu. pastuku	bati

English.	Santo.	Efate.
mountain	wuti	tafa
mercy	koroonogi	na rumien
made last	aa tuptogi	
near	toko velu ki (tana?) tetavwora	milatiga
not	(Wu. roko resi, absent)	ti, tiba, tika
new	awo	fau, d. faum
neighbour	tux, tuom, &c.	nata milatiga (person near)
net	muliu	kokoti
night	pon (Wu. poni)	bog
oil	ruina	naror
old	awe (worn out) meerosi	tuai
orphan	pora	meta busa
outside	pegis	ekatema (outside of house)
obey	meraka	rog berakati, rog na lona
oblivion	limto lie motvanu	miroa gorokoro
overcome	sopsop lo toko	meri matua ki
persevere	ko ao var sopsop tokai	

English.	Santo.	Efate.
pillow	kadialo	uluma
pare	veselī	
preach	vetokī (wiwivia)	fanau
play	suuvia	marogo
pray	lanlanliona	tafisafisa (Christian)
piece	meala	na kat
pregnant	werweri	tiena
peace	ri leli	tamate
paint	loovi (a)	mitiri
pierce	sokī amo mati	soka ia
pour	ee tuogi ; ee towi	ligi
quickly	wuswus og toko	marafi
person	netuua	nata
plenty	purun-puruna moa	i laba
priest	rirop gin masea tuuagin mogu	natamole tabu
possessed	oc	uliulia
pilfer	lo punia	binako
privately	to vevangis	
punish	te kesi	sumati, barati
reach	se sagara	

AND VOCABULARY. 121

English.	Santo.	Efate.
roar	ururia	gua
refuse	til wul ginia pendago; peerago	garei, malo
ridge-pole	wowo lx	na fatu na suma
roll	luunia; edai	fifi, luaki
unroll	teleria	bukisi
remain	totok tea—tx	toko
roast	kon poni	beni
respect	mel melin gina varvari ren ginna	miroaki
restrain	vet lolo oron lepwai	
report	dadai	rogorogki
retaliate (not to)	sap purogi sap repai repan	bati i tupa, sokari
ransom	(poi) lo meuri sap lo meuri (unredeemed)	neti lu
ready	a koro wea wuoni	
reef	mal tup oo	ni sikau
rock	malo	fatu, fat tok, malo

English.	Santo.	Efate.
ripe	supun metua wedwedu tawuse	matu
rescue	siperia pultekonia	bu lua
remember	limtonia	miroa berakati
run	vi	uru
round	alilgona	taltal
rest	mepus	marmaro
raise the tune	lo moig toko	
return it	ko lo ve samai	
rain	usa, us wora	usa
ripe	metuo	matua
unripe	takovane	meta
reprove	owe	sueri
rose-apple	(Wu. keviga)	kafika

Relationships—

father	tata tamana	mama, abu tema na
her husband	kuaworesi	nanoi anena, anauota

English.	Santo.	Efate.
his wife	kan mena	naguruni anena, anaguruni
mother	meme	tete
	tinana	pile na, reite na
his eldest brother	togana	tai na matua
his youngest brother	tesina	taina kiki
his sister	imana	gore na
her brother	manena	gore na
his son	notuna	nani na, na tu na
child or boy	nedura	totau
young	ulwo	busafusa
grandfather	puina	bua, bobu, tobu na
widow	pot nako	malib
sit	(Wu. soko siwo)	toko tan
sleep	(Wu. manoro; Va. metokruru)	maturu
scrape	karkarosi	gari
see	varuo ; vi	le, lo, d. bu
sweep	dodor dara	sera
stroll	lagin to mxor vet worogi	

English.	Santo.	Efate.
speak kindly	vet melum toko	
silence	ko supun te veti	bunuta
sing	lo ne polo	liga, laga
song	ne polo	na ligana
shut	inmewuti (eyes) povgoroa potovgoroa	bunuti
soft	melumlum melum ra ole	mailua, d. mail umlum
sea	tosi; peran tosi (sea-shore;) (Wu. taruse, sea)	in tasi
foam	luluv wun tosi	na letelet
substitute	derdirire; vervi-rire	auli
slip	teda maro	soka risu
sand	one (Wu. perono; Va. ne wuswus)	na arān
stone	sule (small)	fatu
smooth (to)	mosia; wodorla	musi
swamp	wura	moru
snatch	wusoni mea pulte tenia	lete lua

AND VOCABULARY. 125

English.	Santo.	Efate.
shoot	vine	tiba (with arrow)
shadow	nun	na anu na
	nunuera (theirs)	
slow	aligligo ; alig ;	
	moa	taliali, mailua
send	tilai ; til tuogi	tupa ki lua
	pal tuai ; pal tuogo (drive away)	
sink	olo	tiro
spoil	umi venua	sau lua
	orosia verx	
stick	wodiga	gono
	wodwodsiga	
speak	veti ; vetiveti ;	bisa
	vet wus onia	
	tasi vevatoto	
screw	wosgoni	
strength	vilvile suinai	na kasuan
	vasvas suinai	
spit	lolotu	tanua
	pupuros tuogi	
spear	meur ; soki	soka (ki ola)
saturated	wuô	lue
sweat	memxona	tortoru

English.	Santo.	Efate.
swim	lolos	āfa
sweet	tutu nugu ulumia	kasi, elo
bitter	kogona	kokon
seam	turia liwurwuraka	turi (to sew)
some	rume	tete
sponge	vero	
some	vis mei	
smart	kowuswusogtoko	
sore	kodi	bitunu
support	vevan siwo	silei
staff	arara titig (straight)	tiko
salt	tos wusu	tasmen, in tas
sugar cane	tov	na parai
unseen	uropunia	pelu
steer	lo ne wosi	bu seman ki rarua
side by side	var vile	
scold	rivu—rivriv api su api susueri	sueri
short	wowus	mito

English.	Santo.	Efate.
small	tagerigi	kiki
shadow	nuniu	melu
stand	tup toko	tulena
halt	ko tup toko gini	mara toko
sit down	toko siwo	toko tan
shake the head	gilgilo potuna	liglig bau
in refusal	ilopali	
sickness	ususi	na misaki
spirit	temat	atemate
soul	tolmana	ate, or ata na
scattered	toto veva sale	taferafera
steal	pupu ligo api	binako
seek	asea; van ko asea	bilaga, laga, tele
step aside	tup tavu	tale
scratch	karuvia	karu
shine	sosovrogi	mirama, tera (sun)
stroll	mxor	
smile	didinana	muru
sleepy	sap taru ti jinanu	rog na maturuen
seat	tuuo—toktoko	tea sakasakien
surround	kurgur og pot	bati gori

English.	Santo.	Efate.
sun	metanialo (Wu. merai ali; Va. metan maso)	alo, elo, meta ni elo
sky	toloni (Wu. rôntro) wuruwura	elagi
star	madoi	masei, masoei
sneeze	adine	mutui
smoke	osun ovi	na asu na kabu
scissors	lum gurgur oti	te alat
sandalwood	puero	ni eru ni uta
pay ,,	wol gina puero	
swollen	sosola	tub
stumble	ko sus pogi	tokonaki
slowly	ov sale melum ov lan rire	mailua
sad	lolon uli tenesia	na po na i rogtesa, toro (rue)
select	kirogi	meta lua
sorrow ended	ton moti	narogtesan i nu, or i makot
shoes	pokov gin sori	
be silent	sogon ta veti	bunuta
sore heart	lolon kod matea	na pona i rogtesa
stranger or wanderer	leman se sale ne tuua ururai	natamole basera

English.	Santo.	Efate.
scald	pe tun didiria molgusi	
strong	melgonia	kasua
scent	ponponi	na pon
shut	meta rie met tutaru	punuti
sigh	ruruti	maro bur
speaking not finished	uli vevatot simai tor tagerigi	nafisan i ti nu mau
speaking done	vevatot mo moti	nafisan i nu
stood over the house	tup tetagolo san venua	wu-
sea shore	peran tosi	natiki na tas (edge of the sea)
tree	ne kx	na kasu, d. kau
branch	mesana	na rā na
leaves	ruruana	na uli na
trunk	reepena	na batoko na
roots	kerina (pa, great)	na akoa na
bark	kurina	na uili na
flower	virana	buma na

English.	Santo.	Efate.
things	sonu	sera rogo, *or* nalo
transgression	la va korgoroa,	folofolo sa, sigsigleo
transgressor	netuua suinī ro tuua sui rirī (pl.)	
teach	ulul sorai	tafanau
thunder	ururu	tifai
take care of	lomelumtokai	lo berakati
tie	kedai	uti
thatch	ligi venu gina seri gin venua	taki
trip	tigi tigo	
(in) turn	ravravi	biauli
true	tatino	lesoko
think	limtogoguia limlim to tokai	miroa
time (now)	mine	mal na, mal naga
long time hence	tuai ron tuge	tuai
very many days	ponin tarias	naliati laba
taro	(Wu. pera)	in tali

ENGLISH.	SANTO.	EFATE.
touch	teeli pe ko ne leman	meri rogi, kisi
taste	domia, domdom	bami rogi
throw stones	lade	neta ki fatu
thirst	maro ketia	maru, matru
turn	ko veta poria	meraroa, tafulus
tired	rerin kedi polen metavu	maos, taos
throw away	tapaltuoni	neta ki nia
peace-pole	temwata	
tall	perovu	barau, d. baraf, baram
tempt		suru
tread upon	wuswusia	basi
unclean	malgedgeda	milo
untie	munie	rati
unhappy	tenesia	to sa, toko sa
unemployed	toko zi melum	to palo
visit	takataka	ba libi
virgin	susura kēai	na guruni kiki
village	venu uru toko varvile	natokon
vomit	lulua	lua.

English.	Santo.	Efate.
volcano	wut gini ôvi ov merua	na banei
voice	liona	na lo, *or* na lio na
work	wede wede wuswusonia	na uisien
to work	ao wede	uisiuis
wait for	ligotokai	to raki
whittle	dimtuogi	tefe
well	lel toko ; nô leli	uia
worthless fellow	imi api im vet worogi	natamole palo
word	vevatoto	na fisan
wish	taruia	mesau
wonder	os no ki tugala mo wuti	maga
weak	oosuina	mailua
wash	dodovula wodoria crisa	bilosi
warm	tutunu	bitunu
wealth	rum rum lava rudurudu	na soka na

AND VOCABULARY. 133

ENGLISH.	SANTO.	EFATE.
wail	ol mate no tuu tupurogi; te ton polo va kar mati	tagi
wicked	le negavera kan poi imi api; im vet woroki sap lel porapora = oovun lololo lel ne gavera = lol melum	sa, folofolo sa
water	(Wu. re) pe ra; rara?	noai. nifai
weed	kitsuria	but
wipe	mosia	musi. gasi
wound	ne tuuna (turu)	na manuka
watch	wo to toko	bei, lo raki
woman	geai - keai (Wu. levina; Va. ne kepai)	na guruni
write	ultokai	mitiri
worship	ululo	lotu
wind	loni (Wu. lani) lon ser toko	na lagi

English.	Santo.	Efate.
wind, south	welin	suefate (come down from Efate)
do., north	kona	tokalau
do., west	warsaki	
do., east	toka lx	ruatu, tokalau
hurricane	lon lus—lawa	lagi atu
headwind	koroa—woteli	lagi sa
fair	lon tiperia	lagi uia
walk	sursuru	surata
wise	lolo roni	po matua
web-footed	wonwono	gogo
wise men	ro tuua ro roroni	natamole po matua
waves	sola	na beau
war	lus apapi	nafakal, nieru, nāru
worms	ululi goni api	asolat, ula (maggots)

MELBOURNE:
EDGERTON AND MOORE, PRINTERS
FLINDERS LANE EAST.

www.ingramcontent.com/pod-product-compliance
Lightning Source LLC
Chambersburg PA
CBHW020105170426
43199CB00009B/399